Also by Ronald H. Dykes

James O. Haley: Lawyer, Judge, Teacher, Advocate

Growing Up Hard: Memories of Jackson County, Alabama, in the Early Twentieth Century

Fighting the Just War: Military Experiences of Jackson County, Alabama, Residents in World War II

Building Bridges and Roads in the Korean Conflict: History of Company B, From Scottsboro, Alabama, During the "Forgotten War"

"THEY WOULDN'T LET US WIN"

Jackson County, Alabama, Veterans Relive the Vietnam War

RONALD H. DYKES

iUniverse, Inc.
Bloomington

"They Wouldn't Let Us Win":
Jackson County, Alabama, Veterans Relive the Vietnam War

iUniverse books may be ordered through booksellers or by contacting:

iUniverse
1663 Liberty Drive
Bloomington, IN 47403
www.iuniverse.com
1-800-Authors (1-800-288-4677)

Because of the dynamic nature of the Internet, any Web addresses or links contained in this book may have changed since publication and may no longer be valid. The views expressed in this work are solely those of the author and do not necessarily reflect the views of the publisher, and the publisher hereby disclaims any responsibility for them.

Any people depicted in stock imagery provided by Thinkstock are models, and such images are being used for illustrative purposes only.

Certain stock imagery © Thinkstock.

ISBN: 978-1-4759-4376-4 (sc)
ISBN: 978-1-4759-4377-1 (hc)
ISBN: 978-1-4759-4378-8 (e)

Printed in the United States of America

iUniverse rev. date: 8/30/2012

THIS BOOK IS DEDICATED TO EVERY SOLDIER
WHO SERVED IN THE VIETNAM WAR.

Some wars are won.
Some wars are lost.
Winning is preferable.

Anonymous

Contents

Introduction

I had the opportunity to spend over two weeks in Vietnam during the summer of 2009. I remember a beautiful, peaceful country with lush jungles, tall mountains, wonderful beaches, and friendly, seemingly contented people.

Not surprisingly, my impression of the country gained as a tourist is not shared by the veterans of the Vietnam War interviewed for this book. They mostly recall whizzing bullets; helicopter landings under fire; dense jungles harboring unseen enemy; sleeping in a rice paddy or standing by a tree; chaos; noise; tracers lighting up the night sky; fear; blood; and death, among other things.

The interviews with these veterans were emotional for the veterans and for me. In telling their stories, they relived traumatic times that will always haunt them. Until I became involved in this project, I had not been fully aware of what the soldiers in Vietnam had gone through. Of course, I had seen the movies ("Platoon", "Full Metal Jacket", etc.), but I had assumed they were highly dramatized and did not reflect "how it really was". During these interviews, I found "how it really was" to be not only educational but unnerving as well.

So why was the experience of fighting in Vietnam so emotionally traumatic to so many of the veterans? From what I gathered from these interviews, there appear to be several reasons. The war can be described as unconventional as a minimum. For example, World War II consisted in large part of major battles involving huge numbers of troops fighting

1

along a well defined-front, and the enemy troops could be identified by their uniforms. In Vietnam, major battles involving large armies were the exception. Instead, much of the fighting was done by small groups of soldiers on "search and clear", "search and destroy", or similar missions. The enemy wore the black "pajama" dress of the indigent population and melted in with the other villagers when not fighting. In the dense jungles, their presence was only detected by a moving branch or the flash of gunfire. United States soldiers became even more vulnerable targets as they waded across knee-deep rice paddies surrounded by dense undergrowth or sailed down a small tributary in a gunboat. Their difficulties were compounded by monsoon rains, sweltering heat, leeches, mosquitoes, exhaustion, and sleep deprivation.

Then the surviving soldiers returned, glad to be alive and maybe even expecting to be welcomed. World news was not readily available in the jungles of Vietnam, so only tidbits of the opposition to the war had filtered down to them. When they arrived back on the west coast, they were surprised to be greeted by protesters who called them "baby-killers" and such, and getting spit upon was not unheard of. As a result, many were ordered to wear civilian clothes, not uniforms, on the trip to their hometowns and urged not to antagonize the protesters. If they did, pictures of the incident could be spread over the country by papers and television, making the situation even worse.

Perhaps the treatment the returning soldiers received upon arriving at their hometowns hurt most of all. World War II veterans had been treated as heroes. Veterans from the Korean Conflict mostly just returned home without fanfare. In addition to their reception by the protesters, many of the Vietnam veterans told me they never talked about their time in Vietnam because nobody seemed interested or even asked about it. One of the soldiers said his friends didn't think what he had been doing over there was "cool", so they never talked about it.

For all these reasons, is it any wonder that so many Vietnam veterans turned their emotions inward and never spoke much about what they went through during the war? From their viewpoint, they had been doing what they were trained to do. Since most of them were still very young (late teens or very early twenties) and near the bottom of the command totem pole, they were just following orders, not giving them.

Regardless of their reception in the United States, these veterans do not disparage their time in Vietnam. It was a major event in their lives, and many told me they would do it again. Most were upset because they felt that the "politicians" were to blame, not necessarily for starting the war but for "not letting us win it". One veteran told me they were ordered not to engage the enemy or even have ammunition in their rifles on one occasion. Now, over forty years since they served, a significant number of them doubt the war was worth the effort, considering that the war was lost and that roughly 57,000 Americans were killed in a losing effort.

I must admit that I was not a supporter of the war in Vietnam. I still wonder why we were there in the first place. I also agree with many of the veterans who expressed concern about why the United States did not learn a lesson about getting involved in future guerrilla-like wars. The stories I heard in these interviews, though, convinced me that the soldiers received a raw deal when they returned home. I already knew twelve of the fifteen veterans I interviewed for this book, some of them quite well. Without exception, however, I never knew they had ever even been in Vietnam. If this book detailing their experiences has any value at all, it would be to let people like me know that their friends and neighbors may have fought in a brutal war, suffered great hardships, and deserve accolades for their good-faith service to the United States of America.

Some explanatory comments are in order concerning the recollections of the veterans. The great thing about oral histories is that they are the words of the interviewee, not another party. However, several problems arise when putting their stories on paper for others to read. None of us talks in commas, periods, semi-colons, discreet sentences, etc., but these punctuation marks are essential in allowing the reader to make sense of what is being read. As a result, some compromises have to be made in an effort to maintain the integrity of the oral history ("Why, that sounds just like old Joe talking."), while making it more comprehensible and easier for the reader. With these considerations in mind, I have attempted such a compromise on the following pages. Also, all the veterans had the opportunity to review their transcripts for accuracy.

These soldiers were in Vietnam over forty years ago. Most of them went on missions almost daily, and they cannot remember the chronology after all this time. As they remembered one incident, it would often bring out memories of another incident that happened several months before or afterwards. In other words, their stories are often episodic, not chronological. If all of the veterans could recall every mission and firefight, a long book about each could be the result.

The veterans were forthcoming while being interviewed, and often were frank in their opinions. However, I realize some particularly painful incidents may have been withheld during the interviews; in some cases, these memories were related to me but were requested to be "off the record". Several veterans chose not to be interviewed at all because of such reasons as "I don't want to pop-the-cork because I am afraid it will bring back those painful memories", or "I don't want my family to know about my time over there".

Finally, I would like to offer my sincere thanks to the Vietnam War veterans who so graciously accepted me into their homes for the interviews. I would also like to thank the veterans, particularly Raymond Brandon, Jr., who provided names of potential interviewees. Ann Moody spent hours and hours poring over the rough drafts, proofreading and offering other valuable assistance (if that woman had been my English teacher, I never would have graduated from high school). Thanks, Ann. And, again, I would like to thank the Jackson County Historical Association for co-sponsoring this book, the fourth in our series on Jackson County history.

Jim Hayes

Jim Hayes was a "ground pounder" during the Vietnam War. The function of his six-to-twelve-man squad was to "capture, maim, or kill" the enemy. He describes himself as gung-ho and was in many firefights. He also had an assignment in Special Forces that he is not allowed to discuss in any depth. During one particularly bad firefight, Jim was shot five different times and was left for dead and placed in a body bag. This is his remarkable story as he related it to me.

My name is James F. Hayes. I was born February 20,1950, on Sand Mountain and went to school there. I was drafted into the military in 1968 when I was 18 years old. I volunteered for the infantry.

I went to Fort Campbell, Kentucky, for my basic training. After completing basic, I was transferred to Fort Lewis, Washington, for advanced infantry training, or AIT. After finishing this, I had a fourteen day leave to come home. Then I went to Vietnam around October or November of 1968.

We flew over by helicopter and landed at Phouc Bien. I was trapped there for about ten days because the unit I was assigned to was under heavy fire. Nothing could be transported in or out, so I couldn't get there. The reason for the delay was the unit had run across a bunker complex. They had overrun the enemy's position, but there was still some fire. They had encountered a rather large area of the enemy's supplies and armor. After things had calmed down, they were able to bring me in. The landing was smooth because not much was going on by then. Two of us came in that day. I have no idea where my unit was or where I was when I got there. I was scared to death my first night. The unit I was with was Air Mobile, and everything we did was done by helicopters. We stayed about two days to get all the enemy's ammunition and rockets and rifles transported out. I don't know exactly how much of all this there was, but it was at least four large bunkers full. Their rockets were shoulder-held grenade launchers. Then of course they also had RPGs, which are rifle-propelled grenades. We also found B-40s, which are large and are used to fire on tanks and PT boats and things like that. They had no artillery. After getting rid of the surplus, we put grenades in the bunkers and blew them. Then we humped out, which meant we walked.

Air Mobile is nothing more than a form of transportation. Some units use ATVs or trucks, but we moved by helicopter. My unit had nothing to do with the choppers themselves. When we had to move, they brought choppers in, we loaded up, and they dropped us in somewhere else. How we got off the chopper depended on how thick the brush was and things like that. If the copter could land, we would just get off. At times we would use cord ladders or go parallel, which means we used something like a cable and connected our strap to it and dropped in. You used your hands to control the speed at which you dropped. This could be time consuming, so we used ladders more. You could just get down and go. Most of the time, though, the landing zones were clear enough for the copter to land or hover just over the ground. Over rice paddies they couldn't land, so the copters hovered and we dropped out.

We were in the jungles and were called "ground pounders" or "grunts", which just means we were foot soldiers, who are actually the guys who go into the brush or jungle or whatever. There were four platoons, three regular and one which was nothing but mortar. The number of soldiers varied from six to twelve in small squads, but it depended a lot on the conflicts we had, the number wounded, and the number killed. The company might have had maybe 150 total, which would be an average. In the jungle, we would break off unless it was so thick we had to go single-file. The fourth platoon with the mortar was always in the back. If we ran into fire, they wouldn't leave, but put their mortars up. They were our backup.

I was there probably less than a week before I got under fire. It was a small one. On that occasion we ran into a couple of VC. One was a sniper who shot our front man in the stomach. We had to round up the sniper and get him out of the way. Many times we would try to capture them, but it wasn't always possible. Actually, the chances were really, really slim. They would hit and run. The VC didn't stay around. The NVA, or North Vietnamese Army, was something different. When they set up, they set up.

We'd always carried the M-16 in the infantry. It had to be military assigned. Each squad had one of the large M-60 machine guns, which meant four of these per platoon, or a total of twelve, since we had three regular platoons. If you carried it, you also were assigned a .45 caliber pistol. Each person shared his ammunition. We also had hand grenades but they were difficult to obtain. If we did have some, each person would have just a few.

We slept on the ground. If you were fortunate, you had a poncho. We had C-rations, and from time-to-time we got dehydrated food packs that swell up if you add water. There were varieties of them, but mostly we had the C-rations. We usually got the food by helicopters, but sometimes it was dropped in.

Usually we would cover a certain area for a period of time, ranging from two to six weeks. Then they would come pick us up and take us to base camp for maybe overnight so we could take a bath, have food, drink a little beer, then be off again. But sometimes we would go from one point to another without that break.

We were assigned specific activities, and what we were doing depended on what our assignment was. For instance, if recon had discovered something, we would go in and investigate or take over. It might be hills with bunker complexes, ambushes, known trail areas, and so forth. Our main objective was to capture, maim, or kill. I was doing this for part of the time I was over there.

I was what they call gung-ho. I was into the firefights big-time. Another guy and I became buddies and looked after one another. One day our squad was in a rubber complex and ran into a rather large firefight. My buddy and I got separated. At the end of the firefight, he had disappeared, and we couldn't find him. So we went and searched. We found him around two hours later. He had been captured, shot, and decapitated. Both arms and legs had been cut off and stuck on stakes. Part of his skin had been stripped, apparently while he was still alive because of his facial expression. Something snapped inside me, but I can't explain it. The best way I can try to explain it is that I gained the instincts of an animal. It was no longer about survival any more. I was hungry for revenge. I had vengeance on my mind.

That is the gung-ho part. In other words, I wanted to hurt them any way I could and do all I could do. Because of that, my CO called me up after I had been in Vietnam for five months and sent me to the Lone Ranger Recon Patrol, which doesn't exist any longer. It is one of the units you don't hear about. I went through there and graduated number three in my class. I was invited to stay. I have to be careful what I say about what I did in Recon. It is very traumatic. What I will tell you is we had two objectives most of the time. One was search and destroy, and the other was to go in and locate air fields and maybe capture. We did the kind of things nobody else would do. We basically were a miniature demolition force.

There were only eight people in a squad, and there were only four squads. We were treated very special. We had our own theatre, chow hall, and base camp, and we were isolated from everybody else. In the chow hall, they kept liquor on one side and beer on the other. If we wanted anything, regardless of what it was, they provided it. This is about all I can tell you about my time in Recon because I am under oath never to talk about my time there. It is very painful, and I had a severe flashback several days ago and am not completely over it yet. I couldn't sleep even though I took my medicine. I got in my car and drove most of the night. I had to get my head busy. I am familiar with the post-traumatic stress syndrome, and I know what the triggers are. Yesterday was a better day. I had a comrade come by. He is the only one I can talk to about these things.

I was still in Vietnam after I finished my Recon assignment and moved back to my original company. Instead of talking about bits and pieces of all the battles I was in, I would prefer to talk about a particular one in detail. On March 9, 1969, our company was put on ambush just off the Ho Chi Minh Trail, right outside the Cambodian border. Two platoons were in a horse-shoe formation. In this formation, the open end is always on the road or trail you are ambushing. At about one in the morning, I was on the Starlight scope, which is a night vision scope. I spotted two Vietnamese walking down the Ho Chi Minh Trail and called according to the SOP. It was obvious this was a set-up and that more would be coming.

One of the complaints soldiers had against some lieutenants was that they were book smart but not common-sense smart. It may have been in part because of not much experience, but some of them just didn't have any common sense at all. Well, our lieutenant blew some claymores. I grabbed the scope and looked around. We were in an old dried-up rice paddy. I noticed the tree line seemed closer, and I wondered why. As I observed it closer, I could tell it was not a tree line. It was the NVA coming at us, very large numbers. Anyway, the lieutenant called for somebody to fill in the gap in the horseshoe formation. I volunteered, got in the prone position, got prepared, and stockpiled my ammo. Not everybody did the ammo that way. Ever so often you did what was called "clean fire", which is when you shoot up old ammo and reload with fresh. I was shooting just enough to make them think I had used my old ammo up, but I was stockpiling my backpack. In a big firefight, 200 rounds is not much. It doesn't last long. That night I probably had 1000 rounds in my rucksack.

After I got in the formation, a B-40 hit the barrel of my M-16, right square in the middle, dead center. That is the only thing that saved me. It broke my wrist and elbow, blew out the funny-bone, broke my shoulder, and blew out about half of the bicep. It knocked me on my back, and I slid approximately twenty yards. The medic came and checked me and gave me morphine in the stomach. They called in Medical Evacuation, but the lieutenant stopped it because we were under such heavy fire. When that B-40 had gone off, the area had really come alive with firing. The medic thought I was going to bleed to death. I didn't ignore that, but you got to remember I was gung-ho. It is hard to explain, really, what was going on in my head. I was very, very angry. I was in a war I didn't want to be in, I was doing something I didn't want to be doing, and in some place I didn't want to be. I had seen what they did to one of my best friends, and I wanted to destroy them. I didn't care how, just destroy them.

The medic moved me over to the base of the only tree in that rice paddy. Another B-40 hit three inches above my head, knocking me unconscious. It blew a little of the side of my head off, getting bone fragments in my chin, upper forehead, and neck. I was left for dead. I came to and all I had left was my Puma, which was a knife. I searched around trying to find a weapon because there were plenty of dead bodies. I acquired another M-16 but no ammo. I finally did get some and started returning fire the best I could. I got shot in the shoulder, probably from an SKS round which has the same projectile as the AK-47. You couldn't tell which you had been hit with, but the AK-47 has a very unique sound from any rifle you've ever heard. It would throw goose bumps from your feet up to your head, and I don't recall hearing that sound that night.

I kept continuing forward under heavy fire. After I got hit for the third time, I took dead bodies and piled them up in front of me like sandbags. They were dead, and couldn't be hurt any more. I started returning fire again the best I could. The NVA was trying to overrun us. I knew it and I could see it coming, because I had seen it too many times. So I went to the radio to try to call in some artillery on top of us. It was the only thing that could save us, but the radio had been hit. I found the lieutenant; a B-40 had blown him into two parts. The radio wouldn't transmit, so I dismantled it and used Morse code. The artillery did come in, but we were so far out it was scattered and did no good.

Within minutes I was crawling trying to get into another position that was more secure. I caught another bullet while I was crawling. It hit me directly in the kneecap. I think that was the fourth time I had been hit during the battle. It severed my kneecap and went down right through the center of the bone marrow. It was a perfect hit. Since I was on the ground, the bullet must have been dropping. The bullet went into my mid-calf and blew up, blowing out both sides of the calf. That one, I can tell you, hurt. The one in the shoulder I felt, but I sure knew when the calf blew up. It got my attention. I just had to lie down prone. There was a hole the size of a quarter in my britches leg. I pulled the pants back, and I could see it was a mess. But I continued on.

I want to tell you something. I don't like for people to get loud. Yelling upsets me very much. When you are in a battlefield and this is going on, all you got is yelling, which triggers stuff and causes problems. You can imagine the blood I was losing, because several hours had passed. The Cobra copters came in, four I believe, and within two minutes two of them were on the ground, having been shot down. When the other two got hit and left, we were on our own. Some time later I saw "huff and puff, the magic dragon" come through, and it laid it on them. It was an old WW-II prop plane that had four mini-guns, each of which would fire 5,000 rounds a minute, and they had big bullets. It was throwing a lot of fire out. It was really unbelievable. The plane got hit, and I saw it on fire. It left and we were on our own again.

The blood continued to come out. Since this is about me, I'm not going to tell you that much about others. But the medic took a B-40 hit, which took his arm off. I comforted him the best I could. He wanted me to kill him, but I wouldn't do it. Finally, he just ran off and lost his other arm. When he lost that one, he just kept running out into a field as hard as he could. He ran into a line of fire and was killed. He had committed suicide.

I knew the only way I had of survival was to find a way out. I Morse-coded in to the captain, and he told me to get out if I could. Two other guys followed me. We were crawling out. I think I could have walked, but I didn't want to stand up and get shot again. Apparently they saw us because we started catching pretty severe fire. One guy had a .38, and I was out of ammo and had no weapon. The other guy was also out of ammo and had no weapon. I asked the guy with the .38 what he had in it, and he said six bullets. I told him to save three. He asked why, and I told him if we got overrun to kill all three of us. He said he couldn't do it, and I told him to give me the pistol, then. I was not going to be captured. It just wasn't going to happen.

I got some shrapnel, which hit me in the rib cage. Later I found it pierced my lung and touched my heart. It also ruptured the gland that controls the adrenalin. I already had lots of adrenalin flowing, but when ruptured it was beyond anything I have ever felt. It hit me so hard and so fast I think I could have picked a car up. It only lasted a few seconds, and when it went down, so did I, and I passed out. I don't know if was from loss of blood or the adrenalin hit.

What I'm going to talk about now is going to be real sensitive. It won't go away, and in fact I don't want it to go away. I kind of like it. I came to right at daylight in a body bag. I was wiggling in the body bag, and they opened it. I remember the guy saying "Captain, we got one alive". The captain came over and looked at me. I specifically remember him saying he did not want photos of this man, and they didn't take any. I also specifically remember hearing him call the evacuation copter and was told they were full of wounded and too far out and weren't coming back. The captain said if the pilot didn't come back, they were putting the copter on the ground. They came back. One guy in the copter only had a finger missing. The captain ordered him off. The guy was physically removed from the chopper, and they put me on. I could not talk, but I remember the guys on the chopper were saying that I was going to make it. Another one said I looked unreal, like wax.

They took me to Long Binh Hospital. The way they do it in the hospital is that the severely wounded are pushed to the side to save those not so bad. Then they get back to them if they are still alive. They have to save what they can save. The pilot was very smart. He only allowed me off the chopper, which meant I was the only one who went into the hospital. They took care of me immediately. I remember the nurse asking for my social security number and I gave it to her. Then she told me I was going to sleep and wake up better. I did, but it was twenty-three days later because I went into a coma.

When I did wake up, I asked a guy for a cigarette, and he bought me a whole carton. I couldn't figure out why this guy that didn't even know me was giving me a whole carton, because they were hard to come by. A marine next to me said it was because I had made the guy rich. They had been betting on my survival, and he won since he was the only one betting I would survive. He won a lot of money.

I found out later I had passed away during surgery. They gave me seven pints of blood during the surgery. What kept me alive was not anything physical. It was a spirit. I woke up with a different wound and had no clue what it was. I found out I had been opened up and given heart massage. It took me a long time in the hospital. Remember, now, I couldn't be moved. Eventually, though, I was transferred to Okinawa where I had multiple surgeries. From the blood I got, I caught a dose of malaria. All of my wounds became infected and gangrene was starting to set in. That was one reason I had so many surgeries. They were trying to clear the infections up. Most of it did get cleared up except in my leg.

I wound up at Fort Campbell, where they were about to give up on the leg. It was already starting to turn dark. It wasn't black yet but was on its way. They went in and did one more surgery, but told me that I would lose my leg if it didn't work. I told the surgeon that God gave me this leg and that only God would take it. They opened it up and removed six inches of bone and marrow and replaced it. You know how long that takes to heal. The surgery was a success. The leg cleared up.

They put me into what is called TDRL, which is Temporary Duty Retirement List. What that basically did was give me a certain percentage of disability. Then I got a letter from the VA saying that I was still on active duty. I went to Nashville and they put me in the system there. I worked for a colonel in a dispatch office. My job was to be a runner. I carried everybodys' paperwork that was getting discharged and got it all signed by the correct people. One day I was off because nothing was going on, but they called me back in. They told me you need to take care of this. It was my paperwork and was a discharge from Medical Hold and from the Army. The colonel I worked for invited me to his office and poured me a shot of liquor. He told me to go home, start my life over, and forget what I had been through. They got all the paperwork done so I could go home that evening. A year later, I got a medical retirement from Lyndon Johnson. I got four retirement benefits as though I had served twenty years, because my disabilities were getting worse.

After I got out, I tried to work the best I could. I became a welder and got married. Then I got hurt and had to have back surgery in about 1983. After the surgery, I felt different. I couldn't explain it. But later on it showed itself. I started having flashbacks and nightmares every single day. I had never had these before then. There was a lot of stuff that had been hidden in the back of my brain and had come into my conscious. I couldn't even close my eyes because every time I woke up, I had a nightmare, screaming, hearing voices, smelling blood. I was reliving it. Sometimes I would be walking or doing something and have a severe flashback. This went on a long time. Finally, I had one so severe the police had to come get me and escort me to Tuscaloosa. I spent eight months there. I had PTSD, and it had really shown itself. I told the young doctor, who I really liked, to fix me. He said he couldn't fix me but they could help me. I went through PTSD three times.

I wasn't really a violent man but could be if provoked. I did love to fight; I was good at it. Once I got arrested for fighting and was in my cell. I don't know what happened or what brought it on, but I started bawling and couldn't stop. I think God saved me in Vietnam, but I couldn't call on him then. I hated everything on two legs and didn't want to be around them. I thought they had "elected" me to serve in the Armed Forces in Vietnam, and I was bitter about that. I was bitter at the government and at everything. I just wanted all this to stop, and I didn't care how. What happened in that cell was that I was called and saved. When I left the cell, I was different. I can't explain how it was different. I began studying about religion, relationships, responsibly, and on and on. As time went on, He took some of my pain but not all. You have to have some pain so you will remember, but you don't dwell on it, and you don't want to forget the past so that you can continue to move forward. I will have been clean and sober for eighteen years on May 22. I have been a drug and alcohol counselor for seventeen years as a volunteer.

I have physical limitations from my injuries in Vietnam. I have a lot of metal in me. In years past, some of the shrapnel has come up on my skin as black spots and worked its way out. My mental issues are much less severe, and I can pretty much control them. There are many triggers that could kick it off. I contribute my PTSD to my whole service, not just to my time in Recon. Talking to other veterans has really helped me.

Looking back, Americans won the war in one way. Do you have any idea how many Vietnamese were evacuated? It was a large number. Every country got many of those refugees. Some became doctors and lawyers and nurses. Lots of them became important to our society and contribute to America in what it is. In other words, we actually helped the South Vietnamese in that way. We lost the South Vietnam country to the North Vietnamese, yes we did, but we also gained this.

I consider it a privilege to have served for my country. If I got a letter or phone call today saying I was needed, I would be glad to go, despite what all I went through.

Ray Latham ——————————————————————————

Ray Latham was a member of a "search and destroy" unit in Vietnam. The unit would "search" for the enemy in the rugged countryside and in the small villages. If the villagers were abetting the enemy, his unit would "destroy" the village but make every effort not to harm the residents. He was frequently involved in firefights and received a Combat Infantry Badge as a result.

My name is Rayford Warren Latham. I was born on May 16, 1945, outside Larkinsville, Alabama. I grew up on a farm there that was owned by Dr. Rayford Hodges. We were share croppers. There were ten in my family, counting Mom and Dad. I went to Larkinsville Elementary and to Woodville High School.

I went into the military in April of 1964. I had gone to the draft board and asked to be drafted. The man there gave me some good advice. He told me if I went in for two years and liked it I could always re-up, but if I went in for three years, I'd have to do the full three years. So I did the first. I went to Montgomery for induction, then to Fort Polk, Louisiana, for basic and advanced infantry training. Afterwards, I joined the Airborne and was sent to Fort Benning for jump school. After graduating from jump school, I was assigned to the 101st Airborne Division at Fort Campbell, Kentucky, in October of 1964.

In July of 1965 they wanted some volunteers out of my company. They needed eleven but thirteen volunteered. Eleven of us qualified, and they transferred us to the 327th Infantry of the 101st from the 502nd. Then 3800 of us were shipped to Oakland, California, where we caught the USS Leroy Eltinge. We spent twenty-one days at sea, making one stop at Subic Bay, and traveled on to Cam Ranh Bay, Vietnam. We were some of the first combat troops put on the ground.

We got off the ship and got on some landing craft vessels that carried us across a shallow bay. We got off and commenced walking for about ten miles. We dug in and put a perimeter all around. Everybody had a foxhole, and I shared with another guy. We stayed there for two weeks. Then General Westmoreland came by, and we had a big meeting. He got up on the back of a truck and told us he knew we were lean and mean and spoiling for a fight, and that by God he was going to get us one.

After that pep talk, we got back on those ships, and they carried us back to the deep water where we got on some larger ships and went all the way across the South China Sea to Natrang. Some trucks picked us up and took us to an airfield where we caught C-123s and flew up to Pleiku. At Pleiku, they dispersed everyone, putting us in helicopters. I don't really know where we went; I just know we flew a long way. We landed in some tall elephant grass, and then my company had to walk up a big steep mountain. When we got up, we had to dig in, making foxholes. We didn't encounter any fire on the way, although we had had just a little bit in Cam Ranh Bay.

We stayed on that mountain for about two weeks. Then they came and got us, and we went on "search and destroy" missions. I was in C-Company, which had about 180 guys. There were three rifle platoons and one weapons platoon. We were just trying to get our feet on the ground at this time and waiting for supplies to reach us. There was no infrastructure at all. After a while, we went on this one operation, walking all day and night through rough terrain. You could hardly see the guy in front of you at night. We were mostly single-file, especially at night. We got to where we were going at about four in the morning. I can't tell you how exhausted we were. I just can't describe it. After we holed up, we were told a 502nd Battalion had set down in a Viet Cong training camp up around An Khe. We had only been there about an hour at that time. We were told the 502nd was in trouble and we had to go relieve them.

So we grabbed our backpacks and started going back to where we came from. We walked and walked and walked. At times like this, some of the guys would sleep standing up. You had to make sure the guy behind you was still behind you and had not fallen asleep. I actually fell asleep once standing up and dreamed on my feet. I know it is hard to believe that. We had to be quiet and not talk, only whisper. We finally got to where we were going, and the choppers came out. They picked us up and took us to where the 502nd was. We could see the smoke before we got there. The copters dropped us in. We were getting close air support from A1E Sky Raiders, which are prop planes. They were dropping 250 and 500 pound bombs. Some choppers got shot down there. I remember we had to get the pilot out of one of these and put him on a poncho. He had been killed. I think the 502nd lost about fourteen men there.

When we arrived, the VC was trying to retreat. They knew they were out-gunned, but they had done their damage on the 502nd. With the help of the air support and Cobra helicopters, we were finally able to gain the upper hand. I remember how hot it was that day; it was real hot. We didn't have any water left. There were some rice paddies behind us, and I remember we were drinking water out of them after putting in some tablets to clean up the water so it wouldn't kill you. I remember how nasty the water was from what they used in those paddies to fertilize the rice. I don't know how many enemy were killed. I saw several in ditches and in ravines, especially after we pushed them across that mountain. They had already started smelling real bad after a couple of days. I got to gagging, and the sergeant told me to breathe through my mouth, so that is what I did. That was our first taste of combat. I hadn't been there long at all.

We stayed on the move all the time on those "search and destroy" missions, doing the same thing over and over. The company would get through with one operation and go on another. We went on a lot of ambush patrols at night. In these, a squad of eleven guys would go out trying to find any enemy movement. We left after dark because we didn't want the enemy to see us leave our area. After we got where we were going, we stayed there all night trying to monitor any kind of movement or anything to tell where they were. We always left in time to get back to our perimeter before daylight. We were not supposed to give away our position.

"Search and destroy" consisted of going into an area where we knew that the local civilian population was supporting the Viet Cong. See, the Viet Cong was generally from that area, and that is how they knew how to get away from us. They would ambush us and leave the area, which they knew because they were born and raised there. They wore the uniform of the peasant, mostly a black outfit with shoes made out of rubber tires. When the company went into an area where we knew there were VC, we would destroy their food, including the rice, run them out of their houses, then burn the houses. Now I have heard all those horror stories, but I never knew anybody in our company who ever abused any peasants, even though we did burn their houses down. Lyndon Johnson said we needed to win their hearts and minds, but burning the house down is a hell of a way to do it. We tried to take away anything the enemy could use.

We encountered the enemy on some of the missions. Most of the time they would ambush us because we didn't know where they were. They always had the upper hand. I remember one incident when they hit us twice one day. They were in a village and we took it bad. I'll never forget, there was a moat around this village, and of course they were firing at us. We were running out across these rice paddies with all of our equipment and the rice stalks kept wrapping around our feet, so we were tripping in water better than knee deep. The water was splattering from their gunfire. Everybody was hollering and carrying on. We took the village and burned everything down. We could see evidence where we had killed them because we could see blood. We stayed there that day and moved out that night to the place we started from.

The next morning, I kept seeing these individuals who had on white. The VC knew we knew what they usually wore, so in this instance they had changed to white. They were headed into this same village. We told the higher-ups, so we went back to that village and they hit us in same place as the day before. So here we go again, just a re-enactment of what we had gone through the first day. I'll never forget, I made it to the moat. All of us were just wore out, exhausted, excited, and scared half to death with all hell breaking loose. I looked behind me and there was this large snake behind my feet. I remember that snake didn't even scare me. I was worried about the bullets.

The missions might last only a day. You take one village, burn it down, and do what you have to do. I only got one break. They came and asked if anybody wanted to volunteer for R&R. I was the first one to do so. I got to go for five days to the Philippines in November. I was in Vietnam ten months. We almost never had a roof over our heads or any shelter. Where you stopped at night was where you slept, and all you had was that poncho to cover yourself up. Then in November they set us up in a base camp in Phan Rang. We got to stay about two weeks there getting new equipment and new clothes. Our fatigues were just tore up. Everything over there has a damn brier on it, I guess. We were having to take C-ration wire to wire the soles to our boots because we didn't have jungle boots when we first got there. We only had the old Garrison-issue boots from over here. Of course, they just rotted from being in that water so much.

When we were out, we only bathed in creeks. We just pulled our clothes off and jumped in. Of course, we had a toothbrush and a wash cloth, and that is how we took care of our hygiene. Someone would pull security for us while we bathed. When we were at the base camp, they put us up a shower stall with fifty-five gallon drums. The water stayed in the drums all day, and by the evening it was warm. Man, you thought you were staying in a five-star Hilton. While we were there, this man saw my name tag, which later became obsolete because we weren't allowed to wear them. He wanted to know where I was from and I told him. He asked if I knew this certain person, and I said he was my cousin. He had finished school with my cousin in Scottsboro. His name was Fowler Goodowens. It was strange to run up on somebody who knew somebody. Another time, I ran into a guy named Edgar Luallen from Oxford, Alabama, and he said he and his dad used to come to Scottsboro for First Monday. He got killed over there.

I carried an M-16 rifle for about five months, then they put me on a M-60 machine gun. Everybody carried hand grenades and C-4, an explosive we mostly used to heat our C-rations. We were always overloaded, and that is one advantage the VC had. They traveled light. They didn't have anything but their AK-47 and a sack full of rice, while we had all this gear and backpacks and weapons. For the machine gun, we carried 1500 rounds of ammo. Put all of that around your neck and you have all that garb on and you go out in a rice paddy and they start firing at you, see how fast you can run. In our backpack we had a change of socks and a three-day ration supply, among other things. We would pack the C-rations in our socks, then tie them together and hang them around our neck. A helicopter would come out every three or four days and drop cigarettes and maybe some mail where ever we were.

Since we were already out there, we wouldn't necessarily be dropped off into hot zones by the helicopters. However, we were in some hot zones, and all you could hear was these helicopters making all that noise.

I remember this one mission we went on, I don't even know where it was. We went there around the first of January in 1966. We had this airplane that had crashed on the top of a mountain around Christmas Day. There were seventeen guys on it. We did carry what we call grave registration with us, and we had been issued these black bags with some white powder. If the plane had cleared the top, it would have hit the sea. This plane had some Gatlin guns on it. I think it was a C-47, a Gooney Bird or a Magic Dragon. So they sent us up that mountain, and I think it was the steepest mountain in Vietnam. It was slick from all the rain, and we had to help pull each other up.

When we got almost to the top, we started receiving fire. After we got up there, we were trying to retrieve the Gatlins. The place was just burned to nothing. I remember pieces of these guys had been lying there since Christmas, and some of them looked like chunks of coal. There was maybe one intact body that had deteriorated, but you could see the rib cage and body cavities. The smell was bad and flies were everywhere. We helped get the pieces up and put them in the bags and put in the powder. Then we had to walk all the way back down the mountain, carrying these bags. It was just straight down. Some of the biggest pine trees I've ever seen were there. We slid most of the way down it.

A lot of the time we were just walking around trying to make contact, knowing that if they fired on us we had a chance of killing them. What we were trying to do was kill the enemy. We didn't lay back on our cans. We were out almost every day doing something. There is no way to explain how exhausted you can get or what the human body can take. You had to be nineteen or twenty years old to be able to do it. We engaged the enemy about every couple of weeks.

I was definitely in some situations I was afraid I wouldn't get out of. I had some big-time problems with that when I first got home. One incident was when we were going along the side of a river. We called it a river but it was more like a big wide creek. The 1st Platoon was the lead platoon, and I was in the 2nd. The 1st got ambushed, so we swung around to get behind the 1st. When we did, we couldn't fire at the enemy because the 1st was in front of us. I had this Lieutenant Hudson, the platoon leader, who got shot. All hell was breaking out with all the firing. I was hugging the ground as low as I could get and couldn't fire. I'll never forget, I was in a sugar cane field. Anyway, I saw some movement over to my left and almost shot because I thought it was a VC. But something came dragging by me. I hardly recognized it, but it was Lieutenant Hudson. I get a Christmas card from him every year. He knows how close I came to shooting him. As soon as the Cobra helicopters came down the river firing, the VC cut and ran. The Cobras had rockets and Gatlin guns on them.

We did follow up on a lot of B-52 raids, which was part of our mission. We never could hear them, they were so high, but we could feel the rumble. Of course, that was always a hell of a mission getting into where they bombed because it was mostly in the mountainous areas, and we had to walk there. As far as I remember, I never saw a dead VC. The VC that we killed were mostly shot or killed in close air support with 250 pounders or 500 pounders or by the Cobras, but they must have removed their dead with them.

I remember once we went on one of these B-52 raid missions. We saw a large animal like an elk that had been killed. That was all we could find, but no dead VC. I remember sleeping in a crater that was still smoking that night. I inhaled some of that smoke, and it gave me the damnedest headache I ever had.

Hardly ever did we actually see the VC. We could tell where the fire was coming from since it was pretty close to us, but you couldn't see them. What you would do was fire in that vicinity. Light the sky up was about all you could do. Usually they would leave some kind of evidence behind, like blood or something. Our mission was to engage them, not pull back, and report their presence. The time at An Khe was probably the largest engagement because it involved so many of us and included the entire battalion of the 502nd. Most of the time it was just company-size operations. It seemed like they would hit us and just disappear in thin air; they knew the countryside so well. It was so frustrating because you wanted to kill them so bad. Another thing, after you had been there a while, you began to kind of hate the people. They would be friendly during the daytime but they really hated our guts. I respected them as fighters, though.

It is hard to remember specific missions. It was just one thing after the other. But there were several times when I thought I was going to die. You hear you don't get prepared to die, but I was. I was probably more prepared to die then than I ever have been.

When I got back, I would have these dreams that I would be in a rice paddy and would lose my ammo and couldn't find it, and they would be coming toward me and I couldn't fire back. Sometimes in my dreams I would get shot and try to hurry up and die, because I remember telling the Lord to not let me suffer if I get hit. That was my big thing, suffering. I never was injured.

One guy right next to me got shot in the face, knocking his teeth out but not killing him. I saw him about thirty-five years later at a reunion. I had a lot of guys in my unit wounded. We lost a 1st sergeant, who was killed by a sniper, as well as others. I didn't have any close friends who were killed, but some were wounded.

I haven't talked about all of this much because you think nobody would understand what you were talking about. You come back home and it is like, "Where you been?"

I remember one morning we were going out. I noticed this black guy behind me. He was new and had just gotten there as a "filler" trooper. He had been down in the Dominican Republic in the 82nd Airborne Division after President Johnson had deployed some troops. His name was Harold T. Edmondson. I remember him well. He was a little bitty guy. We were walking across this rice paddy, and we received fire. The first thing you do is try to get behind some cover, which was a rice paddy dike. Anyway, he got shot in the head and was killed. He was right behind me when that happened. He had raised up his head and got shot. Years later, I was flipping through a magazine I subscribed to. I came upon this funeral in North Carolina. Lo and behold, years before a photographer happened to be going through and saw this military funeral in process. He got out and took pictures. It was Harold's funeral.

I thought it was ironic that the first night I was in Vietnam a black guy from Selma, Alabama, representing the civil rights struggle, and a white boy from Scottsboro, the home of the Scottsboro Boys case, were together digging a foxhole thousands of miles from home. He would watch my back for two hours, then I would watch his. All this stuff had gone on back here, and we were depending on each other for our lives. I didn't notice any racial problems where I was. You have to remember that a lot of those problems were in the rear where guys were idle and had time to get into these conflicts and things. We didn't have time; we were always on the move. Hell, the next minute you might depend on that guy to save your life. I think "Platoon" was the most accurate movie about the war I've seen because those guys stayed out in the boonies like we did. I would also like to dispel the notion of all the drug activity that was supposed to be going on. I swear that I never saw any drug use from any of our guys. It infuriated me when they portrayed Vietnam veterans as drug heads, mentally deranged, and this kind of stuff. It had a hell of a bearing on me.

It is possible that I killed or wounded some of the enemy. I was involved in two situations that I wish had not occurred, but I was following direct orders. I was young, and obeying orders was part of our training. Now, years later, I would have handled those situations differently. As I mentioned earlier, several members of my platoon were killed. Private Messer was shot point blank in the chest with a .45 by a member of the unit who thought his clip was empty. He pulled the trigger and killed Sgt. Messer. One trooper a few feet from me, Private Moore, was shot in the head while we were in a rice paddy, about the same time Edmondson was killed. One soldier drowned while we were crossing a river. He only had eight days left in the country. After that, they would bring you back to the rear thirty days before you were to go home. They always change the rules after the fact.

The lasting memory I have of Vietnam is how bad it stunk, how exhausted we were all the time, how nasty we were, how awful the hygiene was, how you couldn't sleep because the mosquitoes were eating you alive and had to be bathed in that old repellant all the time. When crossing the creeks and rivers, you had to make sure you bloused, or tied, your pants legs to your boots to keep the leeches off. On the other side, we would take our shirts off and inspect each other to make sure we didn't have any on us. We burned them with a cigarette and they would fall off.

I lost three cousins that I know of in the Vietnam War. A second cousin was there about six months before he got killed. Another got shot while in the 1st Cavalry. The third got killed in a helicopter crash. I had two brothers who were in the service at the same time, and one of them went to Vietnam after I came back. I have a news clipping telling about the three of us serving the country. It's funny because the article said that at that time I was on vacation in the Philippines.

I was over there ten months. I got the Combat Infantry Badge and am most proud of that than anything. The Badge was an indication that you were in combat, so it is a special thing.

When I came back, I went home to Larkinsville and worked with my dad for a while. He was in the timber business. Then I decided to go to college. My did didn't have much faith in me and offered to buy me a steak dinner if I lasted three months. But anyway, I fooled him. I went to college at Northeast and Jacksonville State. I studied criminal justice.

I had worked all the way through college as a police officer. When I got out of college, I went to the Montgomery Police Department and worked there about four years. Then I came back home and bought a restaurant and saw I didn't like that, so I went to work at TVA. Later on, TVA sent me to Georgia to the Federal Enforcement Training Center, which had a high wash-out rate. If you didn't pass all segments, you were automatically terminated. I had about seventeen years with TVA, so I had a lot at stake. But I went ahead and graduated and got my commission as a federal police officer. I worked here in North Alabama with TVA as a federal law enforcement officer. I rode the river and enforced boating laws, doing regular enforcement duties.

Four years after I got back, I joined the Alabama National Guard and retired from there. That was one of the best things I ever did, even making several trips out of the country. I retired as a Master Sergeant, an E-8.

After all these years, these are my thoughts about the Vietnam

War. At the time, I thought it was the right thing to do. I loved my country and put it first. But I despised what I saw developing when I came back home. As the years progressed, I really got bitter, not toward my country, but toward the people in this country who knew we had lost over 60,000 guys over there, including the missing, but were burning the flag anyway. It is hard to believe the hate I had for them.

In hindsight, we should never have gotten involved. I lay it all at the politicians feet. I do think that if John F. Kennedy had not gotten killed, we never would have become involved as deeply as we did. I do not think it was worth the cost. What hurts so bad is that I would not want a parent or widow to know how I feel about it. I hate to think that Harold Edmondson gave his life and of his parents' suffering and crying, and that it was for nothing.

George Jones ─────────────────────

George Jones was a helicopter pilot in Vietnam. These pilots had one of the highest fatality rate of any group in the war, and from his experiences, one can understand why. He was a pilot of both UH-1s (Hueys) and OH-6 (Cayuse) scout helicopters. The latter were used by hunter/killer teams and were flown from several feet off the ground to tree-top level, often drawing enemy gunfire in order to locate their position. George received the Army Air Medal for Heroism and twenty-nine Oak Leaf Cluster medals, each representing twenty-five hours of actual combat flying.

My name is George Henry Jones. I was born in New London, Connecticut, on June 16, 1946. When I was three years old, my father moved to East Lyme, Connecticut, where I was raised.

After graduating high school, I attended college at Thames Valley State Technical College in Norwich, Connecticut. I was in my second year when I entered a phase of my life where I was trying to decide what I wanted to be when I grew up. I was studying to be a draftsman with thoughts of working at General Dynamics in the nuclear submarine design department. During that second year of college, I came to the conclusion that was not what I wanted to do. My father suggested that I look into the U.S. Army program for helicopter pilots he had read about. Although I had never flown in my life, I followed his suggestion and went to visit the local recruiter.

I went into the Army on June 6, 1966. I was sent to basic training at Fort Polk, Louisiana. After completing basic, I received orders to go to Fort Wolters, Texas, where I received preliminary and basic flight training, to include Warrant Officer training. As a Warrant Officer candidate, my pay grade was increased to E5, Spec.5, for pay purposes during the nine months I was in flight training.

I learned to fly in a two-seat OH-23 training helicopter. I spent about five months training at Fort Wolters before receiving my orders to proceed to Fort Rucker, Alabama, for advanced training in UH-1 Huey helicopters.

I graduated from flight school in June of 1967, at which time I was promoted to Warrant Officer as a helicopter pilot. To me, a Warrant Officer was similar to being a civilian in the military. My responsibility was to fly helicopters. Other than this, I had very few additional duties.

Following graduation, I received my orders to proceed to Fort Knox, Kentucky, as a pilot in the 7th Squadron, 1st Air Cavalry of the 1st Aviation Brigade, not to be confused with the well-known 1st Cavalry Division. Our unit trained together for about six months before receiving orders for Vietnam. In December of 1967, we flew our helicopters to Long Beach, California, where they were loaded onto ships en-route to Vietnam. The pilots and crews were flown back to Fort Knox. We took a short break for the holidays with our families. We then flew back to California, were loaded on a troop ship, and sailed to Vietnam as a unit. It took twenty days before arriving in Vietnam.

When we arrived in Vietnam, the ship's first stop was in Da Nang. After unloading troops from other units along with equipment, we sailed south down the coast, making several more stops before arriving in Vung Tau. We disembarked and were processed in, then flown by Chinook helicopters (which look like a pickle with rotors on both end) to our new unit headquarters in Di An, just north of Saigon.

In order for our pilots to receive orientation to the landscape and to experience combat conditions, pilots were temporarily transferred for a few weeks to experienced combat units. We trained with pilots in operations-mode before returning to Di An.

I flew UH-1 "slicks" during my first three months in Vietnam, inserting infantry troops into landing zones or moving supplies from location to location, similar to a truck, but by air. We would carry American troops, Army of the Republic of Vietnam (ARVN) troops, supplies, ammunition, or whatever else needed to be moved. This included soldiers wounded and/or killed in action, which was the most difficult mission of all.

I flew missions as a single aircraft, but sometimes we would be part of a formation of helicopters inserting infantry into an LZ (landing zone). Formations were usually staggered with a helicopter on the right or left, front and/ or back. Formations could have any number of helicopters, depending on the size of the operation and the number of troops involved. It could be two helicopters, or maybe ten or more. Each Huey had a crew of four: a pilot, co-pilot, door gunner, and a crew chief who also served as the other door gunner.

When flying into an LZ in a formation, if you were not the lead helicopter, you would line up behind or off-set at a forty-five degree angle of the helicopter in front of you, depending on the formation type. Some missions would take us into a "hot" LZ. Our door gunners would be firing into the tree lines to suppress enemy fire. We would make a low pass and then go, trying not to stop while in the LZ. We would pass just low enough and barely long enough for the troops to jump out or climb in. During the insertions or extractions of troops from "hot" landing zones, there would normally be several gunship helicopters firing machine guns and/or rockets at enemy locations in an attempt to suppress their gunfire.

My tour of duty in Vietnam was for one year. During my tour, I was rotated to three different helicopter units. My first four months, as mentioned above, were with the 7/1st Air Cavalry in Di An. The next five months were with the 3rd Squadron, 17th Air Cavalry in Tay Ningh, and the last three months were with the 117th Assault Helicopter Company in Long Bingh.

After my first few months with the 7/1 Air Cavalry in Di An, the first unit I was with, and George being George, I became very bored and wanted to see more action. I was twenty-one years old and had that young adult feeling of being indestructible. This led me to make some major changes in my daily life. I had been engaging in discussions with friends who were flying in hunter/killer teams in a smaller four-seat helicopter, the 06-Cayuse, a LOH (Light Observation

Helicopter), referred to as the Loach. The experiences they shared got my attention.

The OH-6 helicopter was shaped like an egg with a tail boom. You see one in the old Hawaii Five-O television shows. The missions of an OH-6 pilot would at times require him to fly along tree lines or scout specific areas, in some cases hovering or even drawing fire from the enemy in order to accomplish the mission. The LOH usually flew missions with a UH-1C, Huey gunship, or an AH-1G Cobra gunship. The gunship provided cover fire-power should the LOH draw enemy fire or it could attack hostile targets identified by the LOH. When the LOH drew enemy fire, it would turn and fly away with its tail pointing toward the enemy. This would help target the enemy position for the gunship to go on the attack.

After listening to my friends' experiences in the LOH, I knew this was where I needed to be. After all, the LOH in a hunter/killer team had a 7.62mm mini-gun, which was a six-barrel machine gun mounted on the left side of the helicopter. This gun could fire thousands of rounds per minute.

After flying Hueys, I finally requested for and was reassigned to fly the LOH in hunter/killer teams. The LOH crew consisted of one pilot and one non-pilot observer who was another pair of eyes. The observer would carry his personal weapon of choice, usually an M-16, a CAR-15 (short version of the M-16), or a grenade launcher.

The LOH flew missions at low altitudes, sometimes just above the ground or tree line. I soon learned that the LOH was a flying target. Drawing enemy fire occurred more times than I wish to remember. I had several helicopters hit by enemy fire during missions, but they all kept on flying.

During our hunter/killer missions, we were in constant communication with our gunship pilot. We needed him to know when something was happening, especially when we were taking fire. The gunship pilot would be in a good position to help direct us when we were flying at low altitudes, such as "go left" or "go right" or "ten-o'clock". The directions would help us navigate or help steer us to a point of interest. The speed and altitude were always determined by the LOH pilot.

The bullet that came the closest to hitting me was during a mission to locate a sniper who had an American unit pinned down. I apparently flew right over the top of him. I heard the shot as it went through the skid of the helicopter below me, came up through the floor, hit the armored plating of my seat, and ricocheted alongside my body up into the door jamb. Neither the bullet nor fragmented metal hit me.

Another incident was when escorting and scouting for an American convoy traveling alongside a mountain, Nui-Ba-Dingh, in Tay Ninh Province. The area was relatively flat except for this one large mountain that shot up to 3000 feet. There was a fire base at the very top of the mountain, and it was continually being attacked by the enemy for control of the mountain. There were tunnels and holes all over the mountain, primarily controlled by the enemy, commonly referred to as the Viet Cong.

I was flying low to the ground ahead of the convoy, checking tree lines and suspicious areas short distances from the road when my observer called , "I see something". I made a second pass of the area when he quickly pulled his M-16 up and fired. Amazing shot. He hit his camouflaged target lying on the ground while we were moving at about 60 to70 miles per hour.

After he shot, we were moving toward a tree line when all of a sudden we had tracer rounds coming at us, passing on the left and the right. I yelled on the radio to our Cobra gunship that we were taking fire and immediately made a 180-degree turn to the right. My tail was now pointing at the tree line as the Cobra started a gun run and opened fire. After completing the turn, I was heading toward another tree line when, all of a sudden, more enemy fire and more tracers headed in my direction. I had been ambushed and was in the middle between the two tree lines with Viet Cong shooting at me from both.

I immediately started into another turn to try and get away. The Cobra pilot yelled at me, "Get out of there". His rockets were on the way to the target, and he didn't want to hit me. I pulled in all the power I had and started to go almost straight up, putting as much space as possible between me and the Viet Cong. Tracer rounds were now going by that looked to be the size of a tennis ball or bigger.

When I finally reached a safe altitude and joined up with the Cobra, the pilot started to make gun runs on the enemy positions. I provided cover for him with my mini-gun as he pulled up, out of his gun run. After several passes, we had to disengage and return to base to refuel and rearm.

Before we had departed from the area, however, the convoy we had been accompanying reported they were now under attack., but we had successfully uncovered the ambush early enough that the convoy did not drive fully into the enemy trap. The convoy was able to pull back while more attack helicopters and fighter jets were en-route to assist. We later learned that the enemy had camouflaged positions about half-way up the side of the mountain and started firing at the helicopters and fighter jets.

After landing to refuel, my observer jumped out to start refueling the helicopter while I kept the engine running so we could quickly return to the action. The observer came back to his door and yelled, "Shut it down! We were hit". He had seen a large hole in the engine compartment door. The round entered the engine compartment from low on the right side, and then made a real large hole when exiting on the upper left side. Only a miracle kept the round from hitting the fuel line or critically damaging the engine, which would have been deadly for both of us.

Missions came up almost every day. We never knew what we would encounter or what the outcome was going to be. We were always on the alert for trouble. I remember one mission when we got into what I would call a fast-draw contest with a Viet Cong. Our hunter/killer mission was to scout an area where a major battle had taken place on the previous day. We were performing a mop-up or clean-up operation. We were flying low when we came upon a small hut, which was a roof on four posts. Under the roof were stacked bags of grain and other farming supplies. We got very suspicious of it and fired several bursts at it with the mini-gun. The Huey gunship also fired a few bursts into the hut, knocking it down. We slowly approached the collapsed hut and quickly saw we had killed two Viet Cong who were hiding behind the grain.

We then continued on with our mission. We didn't fly very far when we came upon another small hut. From a distance, the only thing we could see was what looked like a carpet on the floor of the hut, with a small lump in the center. Not too concerned at what we saw, my observer fired a few rounds into the carpet before we approached the hut for a closer look. I approached the hut with the nose of the LOH pointing straight ahead and my observer's weapon pointed off to the left. I was slowly hovering forward at about five feet off the ground, my mini-gun pointing above the hut. We were looking at the rug through the glass bubble below our feet.

As I flew within about ten to fifteen feet of the hut, we had an unexpected surprise. The rug blew away, and we were now looking at a Viet Cong with an AK-47 lying next to him. We saw blood, indicating the observer had hit him when he fired. In almost slow motion, the Viet Cong started to reach for his AK-47. I slammed the right pedal, turning the nose of the LOH to the right so my observer might have a shot, and simultaneously pulled the cyclic back, causing the helicopter to move away from the hut. My observer started shooting almost immediately, hitting the Viet Cong before he could fire his rifle. I was then able to aim the mini-gun and fire a burst. The fast-draw was over, but we weren't done yet.

We proceeded to fly around the area looking for any friends he may have had. We didn't see anyone, and this is when we pulled a really stupid stunt. We went back to where we shot the Viet Cong. We looked at the AK-47, and we wanted it. To get it, we had to touch down so the observer could jump out, grab the rifle, and jump back in, and that is what we did. After retrieving the rifle, we had to return to the base with our gunship to refuel. Refueling complete, we headed back to the site where we retrieved the weapon. Something looked really different. The body of the Viet Cong was missing. He did have friends in the area who removed his body. We now realized that his friends could easily have blown us out of the air but were reluctant to reveal their positions to the gunship. This was definitely the most stupid thing I ever did while piloting a helicopter. We quickly realized how deadly this act could have been. However, I did keep the AK-47 as a personal weapon for several months before transferring to another unit.

In another situation, we uncovered a stash of weapons in some tall grass. A firefight broke out, and several gunship helicopters proceeded to engage and eventually destroy the enemy positions. An infantry support unit was called in to ensure the enemy had been eliminated. The unit was then able to pull the weapons and other equipment out into the open. Some of the weapons were then loaded onto my helicopter at the request of the infantry commander. When we returned to base, our company commander took possession of the weapons.

While serving with the 3rd Squadron, 17th Air Cavalry in Tay Ninh, which was a large airfield and military compound, my unit had the security responsibility to man several of the perimeter defensive bunkers. The bunkers looked out over barbed wire and areas with defensive landmines. Our location was frequently attacked with rockets and mortars, but rarely an enemy ground assault. On one particular night, during the usual rocket and mortar attack, an unknown number of enemy infantry troops attacked under very heavy machine gun fire. They attacked the bunkers our troops were manning and managed to break through the perimeter into the compound, killing several of our troops and destroying several helicopters with satchel explosives. The enemy troops were eventually killed, including several who did not have the opportunity to set off their explosives. Prior to the sun coming up, our helicopters were taking off on search and destroy missions for the remnants of the enemy force.

Helicopter pilots, I believe, had the highest rate of fatalities compared to other units. During my tour in Vietnam, I lost several pilot friends to injuries or fatalities. On one occasion in particular, my roommate was the pilot on a second LOH, flying behind me on a mission. This was a unique mission in that we had two of these flying together. As my roommate followed me, he made the mistake of flying over the same spot I had flown. Viet Cong gunners would barely hear the first helicopter approach as it quickly went by at a low altitude. But they became more alert, listening and ready to respond, as the second helicopter approached. As my roommate approached them, the Viet Cong opened fire, hitting him in the ankle. His observer was able to help fly the LOH as we searched for a safe place to land. I happened to have another pilot as my observer on this mission. When we were able to land, the other pilot got into my roommate's LOH, and we then flew him to the hospital on base. He was later flown back to the states.

Another interesting moment occurred shortly after takeoff from Tay Ningh on a hunter/killer mission. We received a mayday call that a fighter jet had been shot down along the Cambodian border, which was just northwest of where we were. We arrived on the scene of the downed jet to find a Huey hovering in a bomb crater with the pilot's crew getting out. The parachute of the fighter pilot had gotten hung up in a tree and he was dangling below his chute, high off the ground. The Huey crew was going to try to get him out of the tree. The pilot of the Huey called me to tell me that there was a second pilot who also parachuted out of the fighter jet. As I started off to find the second pilot, I noticed that several Huey and Cobra gunships were now circling. Enemy movements in our direction had been detected., and they soon started to make gun runs on the perimeter of our rescue operation. We encountered sporadic enemy fire during the operation.

In a few minutes, I had located the second pilot. He was lying on his back in an area of very tall bamboo, approximately fifty to seventy-five feet high. He was still in his parachute and waving to us. I found out later he had two broken legs and a broken arm. He couldn't move. There were no clearings in the immediate area to land. In order to get to him, I decided I would have to hover straight down into the bamboo stalks. As I started to descend down into the bamboo, my rotor blades started to cut into it. I had no idea as to the damage this was causing the blades.

When we were low enough, my observer jumped out and started to crawl his way over to where the injured pilot was lying. His progress was hampered by dead bamboo piled several feet high from years of growing in this area. This caused the observer's legs to sink into the pile of brush, making it difficult to walk, but he slowly managed to get to the pilot. It didn't take long to figure out that the observer could not carry the injured pilot to the helicopter without help due to the bamboo. I needed help and called for it.

As I took off, straight up through the bamboo, I left my observer behind with the injured pilot. A Huey pilot responded and located an empty area we could both land in. He said he would meet me there. The Huey crew chief and gunner got into my helicopter. We both flew back to the hole I had made in the bamboo and descended back down again. The Huey crew crawled over to help my observer bring the injured pilot out. In order to get him to my location, the Huey crew lay on top of the bamboo, making a bridge for my observer to walk and crawl on, carrying the injured pilot. When they got to me, the injured pilot was put in the back seat of my helicopter, and the observer stood on the landing skid, holding the pilot in the seat. I had to leave the Huey crew behind on the ground because my copter would have been too heavy to take off with them.

I flew back to the cleared area where we transferred the injured pilot to a Huey air evacuation helicopter, and I escorted the Huey back to the hospital in Tay Ningh. Another LOH assisted in the rescue by hovering down into the hole I had made in the bamboo to bring out the crew of the Huey. The crew of the Huey that was hovering over the bomb crater did manage to get the first jet pilot from the tree. Unfortunately, as they were getting him into the Huey, one of the rotor blades hit a tree stump, causing it to crash into the bomb crater. No one was hurt. But now, the Huey crew of four and jet pilot all needed to be rescued. An Air Force helicopter and another Huey assisted in completing the rescue and getting everyone out.

This rescue operation became a "big-to-do" and was called a "merry-go-round" rescue. (Note: This incident received coverage in the Army Times and in newspapers across the country, including in George's hometown. His name was prominently mentioned in all of them.) It was an interesting way to spend the day. As a result of these events, the Air Force did send me a letter of commendation for rescuing their pilot. I'm not sure why the Army never recognized the rescuers.

When involved in an emergency such as this, it is similar to going down the road in your car and encountering a car accident. If you are the first one on the scene, you jump out and try to help without thinking of your own safety. In cases like the one I just described, the training I received helped make the day a success.

With only three months left in my tour, I think someone wanted to give me a break. I was transferred to the 117th Assault Helicopter Company in Long Binh, just northeast of Saigon. We were flying UH-1, C Model gunships. Our armament consisted of a varied combination of rockets and machine guns. Most of our missions were in support of Huey slicks going into landing zones or in support of military units on the ground requiring fire support. Our crew was typical of that of a Huey crew, including a pilot, co-pilot, door gunner, and a crew chief. The pilots were always experienced combat veterans in the particular aircraft we were flying. A pilot fresh out of helicopter flight school would be the co-pilot until he had enough experience to transition to the pilot seat.

As a Warrant Officer and a pilot in Vietnam, I always had relatively good accommodations. I was fortunate to have a room to myself or share a room with another Warrant Officer most of the time. The walls might be concrete blocks three or four feet high with wood or screening above that. The concrete helped protect us in the event of a mortar or rocket attack. During my last few months, I lived in a barracks environment with other pilots. We had hot water showers in some locations, but you had to get there before the water ran out.

The defoliant Agent Orange was being heavily used while I was in Vietnam. They started spraying with it to kill the vegetation about the time I arrived there. I now have a map from the Veterans Administration that shows the areas where Agent Orange was used and when. The area where I was assigned was in one of the heaviest locations sprayed. In one of my missions, I was flying along with a small Air Force fixed-wing aircraft which was coordinating and directing a B-52 strike. The B-52s would fly over and drop their bombs in strings. My job was to fly an LOH into the area as the dust was settling and perform a damage assessment of the strike. The dust I was breathing in contained Agent Orange.

I did have repercussions from the exposure. In 2009, I was diagnosed with a throat cancer called squamous small cell carcinoma. The cancer was in my tonsil. I later filed a disability claim with the VA. A Veteran Service Officer with the Veterans of Foreign Wars provided assistance in filing the claim. The VA approved my claim in a short period of time.

When I became a short-timer, with only a few weeks to go, my flight time was cut to almost zero. I was assigned to other responsibilities in the compound, such as in operations, or told to just kick back and not do anything to get into trouble. In January of 1969, I was processed out of Vietnam, taken to the airport, and boarded a flight out of Long Binh back to the states. I now wish I had kept a diary of my experiences in Vietnam. I did write letters home almost every day, but they were lost during a move in 1982.

After leaving Vietnam, I had orders to go back to Fort Rucker, Alabama, where I was an instructor pilot for both the Huey and LOH. I was actually teaching pilots how to be instructor pilots. I did this for a year until I was given three choices by the Army. The first two were to go on indefinitely as a Warrant Officer or take a commission as a first lieutenant. In either case, I would be going back to Vietnam for a second tour. The third option was to get out of the Army five months early. I took the early out.

About eight months later, I went to work for the Federal Aviation Administration as an air traffic controller, which I did for eleven years. That career started in the Boston Air Route Traffic Control Center in Nashua, New Hampshire, as a radar controller. After five years, I transferred to Houston, Texas, as a radar air traffic controller. After two years in Houston, and George being George, I wanted more excitement. I asked for a transfer to the New York Common IFR Room at JFK Airport. This was a hangar at the airport housing approach and departure control for JFK, LaGuardia, and Newark airports. From this location, I worked approaches and departures control for LaGuardia. I did that for about three years until my wife asked to go back to New Hampshire.

After eleven years as an air controller, President Reagan fired about twelve thousand controllers, including me. We were accused of being on strike against the United States government for not going to work. The president gave us a notice to go back to work or be fired. As a result, I'm still on strike.

My next career took me into quality assurance, working as a quality engineer with Stone-Webster Engineering. This lasted for eleven years. I was working at the Bellefonte Nuclear Power Plant in Hollywood, Alabama, when TVA made a decision to not finish the construction of the two plants in 1994. I stayed here in Scottsboro and soon started my own trucking business. I retired in 2010.

Ten years earlier, I became heavily involved in the VFW here in Scottsboro. I was elected post commander from 2002 until 2007. I worked my way up to the Alabama State Commander for 2009 until 2010. I like working with and helping veterans, especially those who have health issues such as I had. We help them file health claims and work with the families of our soldiers serving in Afghanistan and around the world who have been left behind and are in need of assistance. We also help veterans in distress and who need assistance, such as medical bills. We work in every way that we can to assist our active military and all veterans.

During my military service, I received the Army Air Medal for Heroism with twenty-nine Oak Leaf Clusters. The air medals and each subsequent cluster represent twenty-five hours of flight time in a combat environment. In other words, I received the Air Medal a total of thirty times, which represents 750 combat hours.

I have heard many stories about the anti-war movement, which gained a lot of support and momentum in 1968 when the American casualty figures skyrocketed. The demonstrators vented their anger against soldiers returning from Vietnam. Soldiers were spit on and cussed out. I was fortunate. My return flight landed late at night in New Jersey, and I was met by my wife and brother. I was never confronted by a demonstrator, then or any time thereafter.

However, I think I do feel the same as I think most Vietnam veterans feel. We were soldiers, and we were told where we were going and what we were going to do. The job of a soldier is to follow orders, so we did what we were supposed to do. We were in combat situations such that we either had to kill or be killed. I did what I was trained to do to the best of my ability and was able to come back alive. At this point of time in my life, I think about some of the things I have been telling you and am thankful I am here today. We flew almost every day, and I was on so many combat mission I can't even begin to remember the details of all of them.

As to re-evaluating the past, I have only two regrets, namely the loss of 58,000 American lives and the lack of commitment by our country to win the war. When our troops are sent into a war environment, we have to support our troops whether the political motivation for them being there was right or wrong. Looking back forty years, I now believe that for any of our troops to die in combat without a full commitment of the President of the United States, Congress, and the people of this great country, the cost is not worth the sacrifice.

Curtis Davis

Curtis Davis was a Pathfinder in the Vietnam war. He would be assigned to various infantry units with the responsibility of taking over all activities related to helicopters, such as radio control and related functions, which allowed the commander to concentrate on other matters. He was also the first to exit a helicopter at landing zones with the duty of guiding the copter in. Of course, if the enemy was nearby, this made him an easy target. Curtis' worst time was a month spent at LZ Dot, which was under constant attack during the entire time.

My name is Curtis Edgar Davis. I was born September 29, 1947, in City Hospital in Guntersville. We lived in Scottsboro, but my parents were from down there. I went to school here in Scottsboro all the way through the eleventh grade. I went two years in Florida to a prep school, then came back here and graduated in 1966.

I piddled around after high school. I worked as a mason's helper and thought that I might want to be a brick mason but decided not to after talking to some of them. So I started out at Northeast Community College. While there, I got drafted into the Army on November 13, 1967. I was twenty years old. They were drafting into the Marines at the same time. At the induction station in Montgomery, they were coming down the line and every third person they pulled out was told they were in the Marines. So everybody was counting "one, two," and so on. I was not one of the "threes", but it probably would have been all right.

My basic was in Fort Benning, Georgia, then on to Advanced Infantry Training, at Fort Gordon, Georgia. So I did the AIT there, then went back to Fort Benning for jump school. I volunteered to be a paratrooper. You had to sign up for this when you were drafted, but you didn't have to if you changed your mind. I got paid an extra fifty dollars a month as a paratrooper, which seemed like a lot to me. I loved it. It was a unique experience. I was scared the first time I jumped, but once you stand and are hooked up, there is no choice. The people in front and behind are moving, so you have to be gone. After the first time, it wasn't so bad. It seemed like everything was miniature down there on the ground, and you were just floating around up there.

I didn't have any problems, but we had one guy who grabbed his static line when he went out the door. It didn't open his chute but slung him against the back of the plane. The sergeant had to pull him back into the aircraft. When the sergeant got him back in, the guy said he didn't want to do this again, but the sergeant pushed him out the door anyway. We had a couple of guys who got injured. If you did get injured, you were automatically out of the program. The ones who didn't make it were put in the "animal house". They were mad because they didn't complete the program. They might really get mad, doing things like throwing fire extinguishers out the windows.

After AIT, I got orders to go to the Republic of Vietnam. We flew to Fort Lewis, Washington, and spent about a week processing. Then we flew to Anchorage, Alaska, and on to Tokyo and Vietnam. We landed at Cam Ranh Bay in July of 1968. We didn't know much about what was going in Vietnam, but we did know there was a war. They didn't give us any instructions about how to get out of the plane, like jump and run or get in a low crawl. And they didn't tell us it would be so hot that it took your breath when the door was opened. When we went out the door, it was so hot that before I got to the processing station, I thought I was gonna die from the heat. Water was dripping off my elbows. I didn't think I could take the heat. I didn't sleep any the first three days because I was in a solid sweat since it didn't cool off at night.

I went from there to Long Binh and stayed a day or two. Then I went to An Khe, which was the headquarters for the 1st Air Cavalry Division. *(Note: An Khe was in the Central Highlands between Pleiku and Qui Nohn).* At An Khe, my orders had me assigned to the 51st Infantry Division, which turned out to be in Germany. So I said I would just get on a plane and go to Germany. That would suit me fine. They told me it was a typo; it should have been the 52nd Division, Company E. I asked what they did and was told it was Long Range Reconnaissance Patrol. The clerk told me it was voluntary because most of those guys don't come back. So I said that I didn't plan to volunteer for it. So the clerk said since my orders were messed up, I had a choice of going to the 173rd Airborne or 82nd Airborne or 1st Cavalry Pathfinders. Somebody said that I didn't want to go to the 173rd because they just got their tails kicked. So I said I didn't know anything about the Pathfinders, but I might kind of like to do that. So they signed me up. It was actually Headquarters Company, 11th Aviation Group, 11th Pathfinder Platoon. It had been the 11th Pathfinder Company, but had been changed from company to platoon. There were about fifteen of us in my unit.

When I had flown into Cam Ranh Bay, I thought it didn't look so bad. It looked just like an Army base. Then I went to Long Binh and thought it couldn't get any worse than that. When I got to An Khe, I saw that it could. Then they sent me to my unit at Camp Evans, which was near Quang Tri *(Note: Quang Tri was very near the North Vietnam border, north of Hue).* I thought for sure this has to be as bad as it gets with the dirt, mud, sandbags, bunkers and everything. Our company headquarters was at Camp Evans. Later the name was changed to Camp Eagle, and the 101st Airborne came there.

I met the guys in our platoon I would be working with. We got a little training there, like what we would be doing and how to do it. A Pathfinders school was at Fort Benning, but of course I hadn't been through it. They indoctrinated us and showed us how to use the equipment we would be carrying. When we got all of our water and ammunition and lanterns and equipment, such as radios and batteries, it had to weigh 120 pounds, and I didn't weigh but 130. It was all I could do to carry it. I couldn't physically just stand up. I had to get on my hands and knees and find a tree or sandbags or something to push myself up with. With the heat and weight and all, I was thinking

I didn't have to worry about being shot. All this was going to kill me first.

They explained to us that we would be responsible for anything to do with helicopters, such as assisting company commanders in their combat assaults, assisting with Medivacs in getting the wounded out, and helping get supplies in. We would be dropped into an area and be responsible for clearing a big enough area for the copters to land and bring troops in. We were a special unit and were exempted from guard duty, KP, and all of that other stuff that normal line guys did when they were resting.

There would always be one of us on the first helicopter in. Once we got on the ground, we directed the others in. We didn't wear steel helmets because they were a hindrance and offered little protection. Instead, we just wore black baseball caps. We would talk to the pilots just like air traffic controllers did and give them basic information like estimated winds on the ground or artillery fire by our side. If there was fire, we would give the azimuth the artillery was firing from, and the max ordinance, which was the arc or maximum height. The artillery was being fired by our troops, which meant the enemy was in the area. There were some "hot landings", under fire by the enemy, but most of their attacks were at night. The Pathfinders were the first people on the ground, and I guess the enemy didn't want to shoot us and scare everybody else away. They probably wanted more of our troops in there to shoot. I don't know for sure, though. I never worried about it. It was just one of those things. We just decided we may not be here tomorrow; it was the luck of the draw. I was thankful for every day that I made it through.

We would be assigned to an infantry company to control their combat assaults. There would the one of us on the first helicopter to come in and the last person on the last helicopter to leave. We would throw the red smoke indicating we had cleared the location. Then we would fly to another location and be inserted there. We would be with that company commander, too. When someone got wounded, we would call the Medivacs in and help get the wounded loaded. Sometimes, the door gunners and crew chiefs of the copters would jump out and help us with the injured. Once they got my rucksack and my weapon by mistake. I didn't have anything; because they had gotten all my stuff and threw it on the helicopter, thinking it belonged to one of the wounded guys. So for a couple of days I was out there with no gun, with nothing.

When we were inserted somewhere, we would stay with that infantry company for up to a month. We would go with them through the jungle and just become part of that company. While with them, we took all the responsibility for the helicopters, such as re-supplies, Medivacs, and combat assaults from one location to the next. We took those responsibilities off the shoulders of the company commanders so they could concentrate on their troops and the fighting and not have to worry about anything related to the copters. We might stay out like that for a month or two weeks or whatever. It seemed like at least a month sometimes. They would fly over and drop us clean clothes. We would just burn our old clothes. They dropped these boxes, and you would just go through and get a shirt and a pair of pants and socks. I tried to change my socks every day since they usually got wet.

For sleeping, we dug a hole every night. If you didn't want to dig a foxhole, you just slept on the top of the ground, but you didn't have anywhere to go if the enemy was hitting you. I've slept in rice paddies with my head sticking up over the dike. At night, we set up perimeters and claymore mines and trip wires and all that stuff. We had observation and listening posts there. If something at all happened, everybody opened up with their weapons until they could determine what it was. It wasn't unusual to find a dead animal out there somewhere the next morning. If the enemy came in and attacked us, they must have dragged their dead off because we rarely found them. If somebody was shooting you, then you would know for sure they were out there.

In certain cases, six of us were inserted to clear areas for new landing zones. The commanders made the decision where to do the clearing. Most of the time I had no idea where I was. I just knew I was in a jungle somewhere. It might be so thick we had to cut our way through it with a machete. The zones were about fifty feet or so wide. Our job while clearing was not to engage the enemy. We were never attacked while doing the clearing. In fact, none of our guys got killed, but we had a couple to get wounded. I guess we were lucky enough to be in the right place at the right time.

We would work with the different units and the different

commanders. When they would come in for a break in secure areas for a rest, we would also come in if the unit we were with did. A lot of time when we were in the rear, we would be sent to little fire support bases to control their air traffic. When we were in Quang Tri, they sent me to an LZ called LZ Barbara, which was on a little mountain top overlooking the A Shau Valley near the DMZ. Several landing zones were in that area. It got cool up there at night. They might have three to six artillery pieces on these zones, and they were the ones firing the artillery support for the infantry. Ships off the coast supplied artillery support, too; these were the big guns, like sixteen inches. The infantry had forward observers who called in coordinates for the artillery.

LZ Barbara was the first little LZ I was on. There were three or four of us assigned to it. My first day a guy said we got a helicopter coming in and they have a KIA, or killed in action. They weren't able to come in the previous night. They were going to tie a long rope around him and hover over the LZ. Since I was the new guy, they told me I was the one that got to go out and untie him from the end of the rope as the helicopter hovered overhead so the copter could land. The rope had been tied under his arms and the weight of his body and the force of the wind from the propeller had tightened that knot so that I was unable to untie it. That was my first experience with a dead person, so I was really shook up. The copter hovered and hovered and hovered. Other guys came to help and they couldn't get him untied either, so a bayonet was used to cut the rope. We dragged him out of the way so the helicopter could land. We didn't know who he was. The only thing we did know was that he had a bullet hole in the back the size of my little finger, but no other signs of injury. Rigor mortis had set in. On one finger he had his girlfriend's class ring.

I don't know how other people were, but it was nerve wracking. I was so naïve at the time and brand new. I just didn't know. Once I had gone out behind a tree to relieve myself. I was just standing there and I heard this thud, thud, thud about six feet away. I asked the guys what that was, and they said, "You fool, they're shooting at you." You heard gunfire all the time at these little support bases, artillery and other stuff, and you just kind of tuned the sound out. The dust was stirred up when the bullets would hit. What I was hearing was the bullets hitting the dirt. That was my first location and my first time like that.

I stayed at this place for a while and then they sent me somewhere else. Then the 1st Cavalry did a division move. We went down to Hue and convoyed by ship to Saigon. The ships were huge. Before we left, the bow opened up and they flooded it. There were four big boats inside, and they would come out to the shore to get us. They would hold six jeeps with trailers, plus troops. Then the four big boats would come back and go into the hull of the big ship. Afterwards, the water would be pumped out. I don't know how many thousands of troops the ship would hold, probably at least three. It took three days to go to Saigon.

People were sent to different places from Saigon. We left from there and went to a place called Cu Chi. While at Cu Chi, they put on a USO show. Bob Hope, Rosie Greer, Ann Margaret, and the Gold Diggers from the Dean Martin Show were there. Thousands of us were watching. It was neat to get to see these people up close. The wounded were put in the front rows.

Everywhere I went you could see that a lot of it had been napalmed. What always amazed me was that in the northern part of South Vietnam or in the southern part around Saigon, the bomb craters made by the B-52s were huge, maybe thirty feet in diameter. There would be nothing left except maybe stubs of trees. It looked like a tornado or something had come through. You couldn't hear the B-52s, they were up so high. We were told they were going to start their bombing run, and it was just a loud continuous explosion that felt like an earthquake. It was amazing. Then we would go into these areas after they were bombed and there was almost no vegetation except for these tree stubs and you had these giant craters. Somehow you would see people who had survived. I just don't know how they did. They might be bleeding out of their ears from the concussion, but they were alive. Some of them may have been in the tunnels. but we never did find one.

I have been hiking for days out in the middle of nowhere, cutting our way through the jungle, and have a kid come up to me and want to sell me a Coca Cola. He would have a little flexible cooler bag with maybe a six pack of the drinks. He'd want a dollar for a coke. They had been in ice at some point, but they were in just water when we saw them. Thinking it might be the enemy, people would be saying to hold on or get ready and somebody would say it was a kid. We found a truck muffler out in the jungle one time, and we couldn't figure how in the world it could have gotten there.

I don't remember many of the guys' names. We were all coming and going on different days and then separated out either by ourselves or maybe two-men and six-men groups. You didn't really get to know these guys like the ones in the line companies did who served together night and day for a year. I have only talked to one of them since then. I did run into Donald Hodges from Scottsboro over there. I also ran into a Barber boy from up around Hollywood on LZ Dot, which was near the Cambodian border.

When I flew into LZ Dot, a small artillery battery was there. A bunch of South Vietnamese Rangers, real tough guys, were also there. Some South Vietnamese soldiers had a tendency to run, but these didn't. But anyway, I hadn't seen the Barber guy since I got drafted. I get off the helicopter and see this guy with a big moustache, and I thought to myself that I know him. He asked me what I was doing there, and I told him I had come to get them out. He told me that this is the worst place I have ever seen and that the bombardment never ends. I told him I would get him on the first copter out, and I did.

There were twenty-nine Americans on that little LZ. We were attacked every night; it never ended. It was rockets and it was mortar and it was machine fire. You name it, they threw it at us. We may have killed up to 400 just in one night. They even overran the perimeter. I think there were three 105 howitzers on that little LZ. What is called the "bee hive" round is the one of last resort. It is made up of dozens of little darts. Before you could fire it, you had to fire a certain flare and yell "bee hive" three times, which is lowering the barrels and is a point-blank deal. When it fires, it is like a giant shotgun filled with darts. Anything in front of it gets it. It's terrible. The enemy's bodies were everywhere, and large bulldozers were needed to dig big holes to bury them in. I got there the day after that event, but we got attacked every night I was there.

As I understand it, the North Vietnamese regulars were to come and take this LZ and turn our artillery on a neighboring LZ, but the South Vietnamese Rangers were so tough it didn't work. Some of the Rangers got shot by the "bee hive" round because they wouldn't get out of the way.

That was the worst place I ever was. It was terrible because the bombardment was so constant. We had air support every day. We set out heat tabs, which were little tabs we lit to heat up our C-rations, so the fighter jets could see the perimeter at night and get right up next to us with the air strikes and napalm. They did that every night, too. I didn't get burned by the napalm, but I was right there. It's like that Agent Orange. I was right in it too, but I don't know if it has caused any health problems.

The company commander there was in TOC, which is the Tactical Operations Center, and was the most fortified position in the support base. Everybody has their flak vests on and their steel pots and all that stuff. Rockets are coming in. As soon as you hear them, they explode and you don't have time to react. Those 122mm rockets come in fast, too. Anyway, the commander was down in the TOC directing artillery fire and everything in this hole in the ground. There were 12x12 beams overhead, and on top of these were inter-connecting steel plates covered by sand bags with additional layers of steel and sand bags. All of the rest of us just had little bunkers, you know. Anyway, the commander was on one knee with his head down and these rockets are coming in. One hits a beam and it cracks in the middle and falls. It lands on his head and back. Of course, it broke his neck and killed him.

One night some guys had guard duty and were manning the howitzers. One of them was sitting with his back to the parapet wall, which was sand bags around the howitzer. A rocket hit the parapet wall and blew his arm off at the shoulder. He had the arm that was blown off in the other hand, and he was running. Every time his heart would beat, it would shoot a stream of blood the size of my thumb. I've never seen anything like it. The medic chased him down and got a clamp some way on that artery and managed to stop the bleeding. We got a Medivac copter in, and he lived. The medic said if he hadn't caught him when he did, his heart would have pumped all his blood out.

Then another night at the same location, we were in the bunker and being attacked. When the rockets and mortars are coming in, all you can do is hunker down behind something. We were all in this bunker, and a guy comes in and said he had been hit, and one of the guys asked where. He said in the head. They took his helmet of, and he had some blood trickling down, which didn't seem very bad. Then he fell down and when we rolled him over, we saw that it had cut his jugular vein and he didn't know it. He hadn't felt that; he had felt something else. He died instantly. He was in artillery. I was the only Pathfinder there at that time.

Like I said, my job was to take care of the helicopter landings and all. Once at LZ Dot, we had a Cobra helicopter firing on the perimeter of the LZ. One of his rocket pods broke off and fell down but it was still connected, and when he fired, it blew his own rotor blades off. All he had left were some real short blades. I was talking to him on the radio and he said he was coming in but he didn't have enough blade to make it fly. The copter hit the ground, went back up, then back down and fell over on its side. But the two guys in there were okay.

Another time we had a Chinook coming in with a re-supply of water and some new troops. I was talking to the pilot on the phone and asked if he knew one of his engines was on fire. The Chinook was a two-rotor copter with turbo engines on the sides at the back. The pilot said he knew he had a motor on fire but was going to drop the water, which was in 500 gallon tanks made of rubber. One of my jobs was to hook and unhook things that were dropped down from or pulled up into the copters. He said he would go across at about fifty feet and just drop it but that he couldn't because the South Vietnamese troops were in the way. So I told him to drop it anyway. It bounced when it hit, and the water just exploded. He asked me how many of the South Vietnamese he got, and I told him none. Anyway, the helicopter goes out and makes a turn. I told him his left engine was on fire, too, and that he was going down. He was not where he was supposed to be, and I told him he had to get the copter up. The door gunner in the copter was standing there and could hear the conversation on the radio. He was standing there looking at me. The gunner flips his M-60 out the window. The pilot tries to land outside the perimeter and hits a tree. As soon as he hits, he flares the front of the copter up and goes in backwards. Big tree limbs and debris are flying in the air. We go running out there, and out come the troops and the crew. A lieutenant comes out and has his .45 drawn. He thinks the South Vietnamese who are trying to help were the enemy, and he's telling them to halt or he will shoot. The funny thing was that he didn't have any bullets. Nobody was killed. It was funny in a way. Nobody wanted to come into LZ Dot. It was dangerous, and the pilots knew I was the only Pathfinder there. When I was guiding the helicopters in by radio, I would be standing outside the bunkers.

While I was there, we had Thanksgiving turkeys that had been dropped for us. The South Vietnamese soldiers stole our turkeys, and they got caught. Their commander dug like a 6x6x8-foot deep hole and put those soldiers in it with some steel caging over the top. He kept them in there about a week. It was so hot down in there that you kind of felt sorry for them.

Every day, mostly at night, there were bullets flying and rockets and mortars coming in. Mortars we didn't mind too much. You could hear them when they were fired. It makes a unique sound, and in a few minutes it's gonna hit somewhere. When it does hit, then you know, well okay, they missed us, and then they would fire another one. You could even tell which way they were walking the mortars and actually move out of the way of those things if the first one didn't get you.

I stayed at LZ Dot a couple of months. As a matter of fact, I was the only Pathfinder there. I don't know whether they forgot me or not, but I didn't have any food. After they pulled the artillery unit out, I was the only American left. I was there for about a week after they left, leaving me with the South Vietnamese soldiers. I guided the copters out, which was my job, but I didn't leave. I didn't have any food, and I thought they would send me something tomorrow, but they didn't come, and that kept up for days. I looked through everything I had, but I didn't have crackers or anything. In the meantime, the South Vietnamese soldiers were offering me food, but it was rat stew or it was some old green-looking stuff or brown rice, and I just couldn't eat it. I turned it down the first two days, but by the third day I was hungry. You will eventually get hungry enough to eat anything. I had thought I was going to starve to death. They finally got me out of there, and the bombardment had still been going on every night.

One time I was at another LZ, and I was with a couple of other guys who were training a new man. An artillery round from another support base was fired in the wrong direction. We were standing on the top of the bunker, not in it. This round hit the bunker. We thought it had exploded because we were all covered in dust. It was loud and had a shattering feeling. We were looking around to see if anybody was hurt, and they weren't. We came to find out that the round didn't go off. It was a dud. If it had gone off, it would have killed us all, because it had hit right in the middle of us.

There were other times when we were out in the field or in the jungle and we would be overrun by the enemy. This happened when I was with one of the infantry units, and it occurred more than once. They would come through the lines, and there was chaos. It's dark, and the artillery would have to be called in. On one particular night, we were being overrun like that, and we had to call the artillery in. What you do, you get down in your hole and the forward observer gives our coordinates to the artillery. Anybody not down in the hole gets a blast from the artillery rounds. But there is a chance that the round can go into your hole, and that happened in the hole next to me and blew this guy's foot off about half-way between the knee and ankle. They pumped him full of morphine. I don't know if he was feeling any pain or not. He was smoking a cigarette and laughing and carrying on. He said "I'm gonna get to go home!" It was that bad over there. I've seen the morphine given many times. I don't know that it stops the pain, but they don't care.

It happened on more than one occasion that someone wounded would have to be extracted during the night. During the day, we carried these panels like vinyl that you could use to make an X on the ground that could be seen from the air. But at night we had to use batons, which are lighted flashlights like are used at the airports. You had to light those batons and stand out there with the batons so the copters could spot you. Once they spotted you, they could be guided in with the batons. I did this, and I was a perfect target. But if you have someone like the guy who got his leg blown off, you don't think about that.

I was in Vietnam for a year and two days. I did have R&R for one week after about nine months. For that nine months, I had constantly been involved with my mission except for the short breaks that we had to relax and rest and get ready for our next trip out. During each break, I had to get all my stuff ready and packed. I carried six lanterns with six-volt batteries, and you know how heavy those batteries are. They probably weighed two or three pounds each and were about a foot long and a couple of inches thick and three inches wide. I had my radio with a battery in it, which was a PRC-10, along with three extra batteries for it. We carried six quarts of water, grenades, smoke grenades, six bandoliers of ammunition for a rifle, our poncho, poncho liner, and our personal supplies like underwear and socks and things like that. I also had a short antenna and a long 292 antenna which gave greater range. We also had to test everything before we left. We carried all that everywhere we went.

When we were in the field with the infantry, I never had to walk point because I had those other responsibilities. They didn't want the Pathfinders out front getting shot because we were needed for other things. Otherwise, we did everything else every infantryman did, including clearing through the jungle and all that other stuff.

Once there was a mortar attack, and everybody was in the bunker. The lieutenant was coming out the door and the other guys were behind him. A rocket hit right in front of him, killing him. The blast went through him and hit the guy behind, wounding him. I was told about this but didn't see it.

About the last fifteen days, they pulled us back to the rear area, and we didn't do much of anything. They don't want you to get killed just before leaving for home. At least they did us that way. When I got back to the states, I had less than 120 days left. My MOS was 11B4P initially but when I became a Pathfinder it was 11B4Y. When I rotated out, my tour of Vietnam and my tour of service ended. So I flew into California and came back home in July of 1969. There were folks at the airport in California who jeered and spat at us and yelled comments, but we were told to just ignore them, and we did. I was in my military uniform. The people on the planes coming home were very nice.

When I got home, they told me to go by the Veterans Affairs Office and let them know you are home. I had some benefits like the GI Bill. I was also told to sign up for unemployment. I drew that from July to September. I worked at Dunlop in Huntsville for a year or two. Then I went back to school and also spent nineteen years in the National Guard. In 1976 I came to work for the city as construction superintendent. When I finished at Northeast, I took city planning courses at A&M. I was made Community Development Coordinator and later a department head as Director of Community Development. I retired in 2009 after thirty-three years with the city.

In summing up my experience in Vietnam, it was horrific and awful. I'm lucky to be here. From a personal standpoint, I think the war was worth it because it helped me grow up and take personal responsibility. But the war itself seems to me to be for nothing. It was a political war, and they didn't let us take care of business. In some cases, we were not allowed to fire unless we were fired on. We always had to be careful with this. It was almost like we weren't allowed to win, even though it seemed like we had everything we needed to take care of business. I believe politics got in it, and it seemed to be for nothing, just a waste.

When I got drafted, I thought I was invincible and didn't worry about dying. But I got over there and realized it could happen to me any time. The first month or so, I was scared to death. Then my attitude changed, and I didn't care and didn't worry about it. I didn't think I would make it home anyway. The last month or so, I got scared again. I had made it so far and didn't want to die then.

Keith Smith

Keith Smith spent a year in Saigon as an MP. The first 348 days were fairly quiet, relatively speaking. Then chaos ensued when the Tet Offensive began, and he describes his last seventeen days as "bad". Over one-half of the 300 MPs in Keith's unit were killed during the Offensive.

My name is Numon Keith Smith. I was born February 5, 1947, in a hospital in Fort Payne, Alabama. My parents lived in Section, and I grew up there and graduated from Section High School. Immediately after graduating in 1966, I joined the Army.

Everybody knows I was a policeman for the city of Scottsboro for thirty-six years and Police Chief for twenty-six of those years. Most don't know, though, that I got into law enforcement through the back door. After graduation, having never drunk an alcoholic beverage, a friend and I decided to go over to Huntland, Tennessee, to buy some beer. We bought a six-pack apiece. On the way back to Scottsboro, we were stopped and arrested because of the beer. A plea agreement was reached that if I joined the Army, the case would be dismissed. Upon enlisting, I was guaranteed a position in the Military Police. So I went from an outlaw to law enforcement in a short time. The agreement had changed my life.

I did my basic training in Fort Benning, Georgia, then transferred to Fort Gordon, Georgia, for MP training. At Fort Gordon, we began to get a real understanding of what we were about to face. Most the training personnel were Vietnam veterans, and they understood the importance of training and how it might be what kept you alive. Most military people have to credit those training officers with teaching them the basics for survival in tough situations, even if you didn't realize it at the time of training. After completion of MP training, we received orders to go to Vietnam. Those orders were the major change in life's direction for a young man who had barely been out of the state of Alabama.

I reported to Oakland, California, and the next day flew out to Vietnam, along with hundreds of other soldiers. We landed in the Philippines to refuel, and we were allowed to get off the plane for a short time. While there, we could see hundreds of camouflaged jets and other aircraft. This made everything real for the first time. We then flew to Vietnam and landed at Ton Son Nhut Air Base, just outside Saigon. For someone who had never been anywhere much, and not knowing what to expect, arriving in Vietnam slapped reality in my face. People who had been there a long time would tell stories about what they had been through. We knew we had a long year ahead of us if they were telling the truth.

I was assigned to the 716th MP Battalion and stationed in Saigon. We were located in Cholon, which was on the opposite side of Saigon from the docks. The main street was nine miles long. That street was called "the land of a thousand bars and a million bar girls". Our responsibility was to handle conflicts between the military and Vietnamese; to work wrecks between military convoys and civilians; guard officer and enlisted quarters; and guard military facilities such as the motor pool, PX, and dozens of others. Our mode of transportation and patrol was a military jeep. Each patrol vehicle was operated by a military policeman, an infantry specialist, and an infantry sergeant.

It didn't take long to figure out that the Vietnamese people did not look at life as we do in the United States. Most likely due to having been born and raised with fighting all around, life just didn't seem to have the same value as what we were used to. Once, while on patrol, I observed a Vietnamese woman dragging a small girl. She stopped, picked up a brick, and hit the child in the head. There was nothing we could do, because no military personnel were involved. On many occasions, military convoys would travel through Saigon, often getting into accidents with Vietnamese vehicles involving serious injuries or death. Sometimes, the commander of the convoy would negotiate a cash settlement with relatives of those involved in the incident. Looking back, it appears that life was worth what could be negotiated on the side of the road.

As an MP unit, we were required to work twelve hours a day, seven days a week. We changed from night shift or vice versa once each month. We got one day off after the shift change to prepare for the next shift. As Military Police, we were responsible for maintaining control over military personnel. Some were deserters and just mean, but most were regular guys who had an opportunity to get away from the jungle for a short time. Drug use was not something that was openly done, but alcohol use was extensive. A GI would go into a bar, any bar, and fifteen to twenty beautiful young women would be in there. They would sit with him, and he would buy them a drink called Saigon Tea, which contained no alcohol and cost around two dollars. As long as the GI would buy the drinks, a girl would sit with him. Prostitution was inexpensive, also, just a couple of dollars. The houses where the prostitution took place might have as many as ten to fifteen girls. As one could imagine, it was in one of these areas where we frequently had problems. This was just a way of life for thousands of these Vietnamese girls. It was not against military rules to participate in these activities as long as you didn't get into trouble. Military personnel were cautioned to take precautions against venereal disease. However, most drunk soldiers didn't really care about that at that moment.

As an MP, I had to go into bars and break up fights. Since the guys had been out in the field, when they came in they really wanted to have a good time. So if you tried to break up a fight, you could have a fight on your hands, too. There was no gun fighting or knife fighting, just fist fighting. Most of them were so intoxicated they couldn't much hurt anybody, anyway. I recall once we were going by an alley one night and heard somebody holler. We stopped and went back. For some reason, a GI had been running, maybe because he had been in a fight. He tried to get over a fence with spikes on top. One of the spikes had gotten stuck in his leg, and he was hanging upside-down on the fence with the spike in his leg. He was in a mess. We had to get medical personnel, because he might have bled to death. It helped that his leg was up and his body down, which kept him from bleeding as much. Strange things were not uncommon over there.

After a while, handling the situations with these guys got to be routine. But all of them were tense because you didn't know who you were dealing with. If some Vietnamese people were involved with a GI, it might even be a Viet Cong, because they all looked the same. In that respect, it could be even more dangerous. We did have some MPs get hurt, but I never was. Sometimes, I think I live with a protective shield around me, and it was the same with civilian police work. I never acted like I was afraid. If we showed a presence over there, the fight or problem would usually end. Besides, we could get big numbers of military police there if we needed to. I don't ever recall seeing an officer involved in these types of situations. It was mostly lower level guys who got into trouble. Usually the higher-ranking enlisted men weren't involved, either, because they had learned how to deal with all that stuff. The young ones were usually who caused all the trouble.

When we were not working, we stayed at our quarters, a hotel in Cholon called the Capital Hotel. We ate there, exercised there, and prepared for the next shift. It was completely surrounded by a high wall for protection and was guarded by military policemen.

While in Vietnam, you got close to those you served with. I was an only child, so I never had a brother. If I had had a brother, I believe it would be the same as those I served with over there. On more than one occasion, one of them might save your life, and you try to do the same for them.

On one occasion early in my tour, I received an unexpected visit from one of my first cousins, Bobby Bradford. He was a mortician in the military. He had just returned from Laos where a group of his company had gone to retrieve the bodies of missionaries who had been massacred by the Viet Cong. They had brought the bodies back to the mortuary in Ton Son Nhut. He and I spent twenty-four hours together before he went back to his post. As I mentioned, the military police guarded the mortuary. Each time I was there, it was full. After seeing all the bodies that came into the morgue, I often wondered if the number of Americans that were reported as killed was under-reported.

Overall, being an MP in Saigon was much like being a policeman in the United States today, but all that changed when the Tet Offensive hit. During that day, before the Offensive started in the night, the Vietnamese people were celebrating their New Year with fireworks and partying. As it started to get dark and we were preparing to go to our assignment, rocket-type fireworks were going up everywhere. Rifles were being shot into the air with tracers every four or five shots. This was nothing out of the ordinary for that time and place. Just after dark, we left to assume our assigned post for the night. I had drawn the Post Exchange, which was approximately one block big. A tall fence completely surrounded the facility. I was on my post there when it all hit the fan.

You could hear it starting on the radio, with people screaming that they were being attacked. You could tell that whoever was talking got killed. It just went on for hours and hours. I was in the Post Exchange by myself. You talk about growing up; I was pretty scared. I got relieved in the early morning hours, and that morning more people were put in the Exchange. The next few days, we worked twenty-four hour shifts.

I didn't have to be told what was going on. You could hear it. All the time, we had twenty-five of us on call, and if anything happened, we would go out and take care of it. Then another twenty-five were always on call as backup, making a total of fifty. One of the first things happened at the officers quarters in Ton Son Nhut. Two military police were there. At the gate was a big concrete barricade with a metal umbrella over the top, and it was the only way to get in. Those two guards were attacked, and they called because they were being shot at. A task force was sent there that was led by a 2nd lieutenant who had only been in Vietnam for a couple of weeks or so. Well, he was going to take the task force through a back alley to get to the back of the officers quarters. The enemy was waiting for them on buildings on both sides of the alley. They threw grenades down and shot and killed most of the task force. Those not killed lay there all night until daylight due to the intense gun fire from the Viet Cong.

Many other places were also hit during that night, including the US Embassy, Ton Son Nhut Air Base, and the MP headquarters. Numerous civilian targets were also hit by claymore mines in front of motels and government offices. Some government officials were assassinated. This period of time was complete chaos, and it was just a matter of trying to survive until some semblance of order could be re-established.

The American Embassy was one of the most important targets that was hit that first night. The embassy took up one whole block. In the middle of each side was an MP guard-post manned by two MPs. Somehow, the enemy got behind all four guard-posts and killed the guards, giving them access to the embassy grounds. The US ambassador was upstairs in the embassy building when the Viet Cong broke in. An MP who had recently transferred to Saigon from the 101st Airborne was the first to arrive. He went inside the embassy grounds and killed a number of Viet Cong that he encountered on the grounds. He started toward the entrance of the embassy building and observed the ambassador on the upstairs balcony. The VC were coming up the stairs, so he threw the ambassador his .45 caliber pistol, then went inside to confront the remaining VC. There is no doubt this one MP was responsible for saving the ambassador's life and that of others who were in the building. I was at the embassy mid-morning and remember seeing dead VC and dead military police everywhere.

Most of the time during this period, I was in a patrol vehicle with two infantrymen who had machine guns, and they didn't take any chances. Everywhere was under strict curfew; no one was supposed to be out. It was almost as if what was happening was not real. Just every little bit, someone would call in about something going on. A group of us would go there from all directions. It might have been somebody getting shot at some living quarters or whatever. This was just constant and went on for days and days. The people I was with killed a lot of VC, and a lot of infantry and military police were killed in the process. The Viet Cong were good at what they did because they had been doing it for generations.

When we were out patrolling, our forces would bring in those big planes that shot ammo that would cover every square inch of a football field. You could hear the plane when they brought it in, and the whole city block would be leveled. You could go by, and nothing would be left. I don't understand how a gun could do that much damage.

There was a motel being built across the street from our quarters. Several stories had been built, and others were being completed. A sniper was shooting from over there into our hotel. We were shooting back in the vicinity we thought it was coming from. Our grenade launchers were tearing that place up. I think seven of the VC were killed when our forces were finally able to enter the building. One large motel several blocks from where we stayed was destroyed completely when the VC set claymore mines off in front of it. Many people were killed in the explosion.

There were pictures in all the magazines of the Vietnamese general killing a VC by shooting him in the head. I was in that block when it happened. It was reported to us that the VC had killed the general's wife and children just prior to the shooting. This and the picture of the little girl running down the street with her clothes burned off from the napalm were two of the most dramatic pictures I can remember of the war.

On one occasion during the Tet Offensive, I was patrolling the Ton Son Nhut area in mid-afternoon. At that time of day, people were allowed to move around, but we were suspicious of most everyone. An old man came by us riding a bicycle. An infantry soldier who spoke Vietnamese was near us and yelled for the old man to stop. He didn't stop, so he was told again. When he still didn't stop, the soldier fired at him with a .45 caliber pistol, striking him in the upper arm. The old man fell to the ground, and a Vietnamese policeman went over to him, took his ID away from him, put it in his pocket, and walked away. There he lay, shot, with no ID. You don't have to imagine what they did to him with no ID. He probably was considered to be a VC, and he may have been, but I feel sure his situation came to a bad end.

On several occasions, I was around the Ton Son Nhut Air Base, and each time outside the fences you would see dozens, maybe even hundreds, of dead VC lying on the ground where they had been killed the night before while attacking the base. Security at the base, jets, and helicopters were used to turn them back. The next day they would still be there. Some would have nails through their feet, and you wonder how they could even walk like that, much less fight. The reason was they were so doped up they felt no pain. When mortally wounded, it took a long time for many of them to die. The nails resulted from bombs they had made and detonated. Then they ran through the debris, feeling no pain when they stepped on the nails.

Prior to the Tet Offensive, we were not subjected to the harsh conditions and constant fighting like those in the jungle. Then Tet hit, and every minute became a will to survive. It was bad. Our situation changed from police enforcement and security to street fighting and regaining control of the city. We were young, and even though we had been there for almost a year, we were not prepared for what hit us during Tet. Over 300 of us were in our group, and over half were killed in the Tet Offensive. The VC had been fighting for years, and they just about wiped us out that first night. After that, we regained our composure and got it back together. We handled it after that.

I should have been scheduled to return to the States around this time; however, due to the chaos, it was unknown when I would leave. My folks got word that I was missing and presumed that I was dead. I finally got to leave, and when we stopped in Hawaii for a short period of time, I was able to use a pay phone and call my mother. That was the first time that she knew I was alive. I had not known they thought I was dead. I really shocked her.

A lot of Vietnam veterans were affected by what they saw and had to do over there. Most of us were not prepared for what we saw and did. Most of us came home, able to carry on a normal life. Some couldn't, and others didn't come home at all. If there was one regret, and I think most veterans feel this way, the action in Vietnam was not a conflict, it was a war.

After forty years, I guess I think that the military leaders wanted to win the Vietnam War. The politicians wouldn't let them; instead, they were willing to settle for a draw or a loss, and this political game got a lot of people killed in a losing cause.

Raymond Brandon, Jr.

Raymond's job description when he was sent to Vietnam was clerk/typist. However, when he arrived, he was assigned to an advisory team working with scout dogs that were trained to detect enemy personnel and other dangers. Raymond's small squad, usually composed of six or so soldiers, had the assignment of going out into the jungles, mountains, and rice paddies to search for enemy troops and movements and report what they found. If only a small number of VC were spotted, they would engage them in a firefight.

I am Raymond Brandon, Jr. There is no middle name. I was born December 14, 1945, in Scottsboro at the old Hodges Hospital. I grew up here and went to Scottsboro High School. After high school, I went to Florence State Teachers College, which is now UNA, for a year and a half; then to trade school. I graduated from John C. Calhoun trade school in Decatur after training to be a machinist. After that, I went to work for Cornelius Company here in Scottsboro. Before they closed, I was drafted into the military.

The day I left to go in the Army was January 23, 1968. I did my basic training at Fort Benning. Then I had to report to Fort Dix, New Jersey, immediately following graduation for jungle training. Areas were set up like villages and jungles and everything. It was almost like being in the jungle. You had to go in and secure villages, do sweeps, check for mines, and everything else that we did in Vietnam.

After that was finished, I came home for fifteen days, and then had to report to Oakland, California. I'll never forget that every morning at seven o'clock and every evening at four o'clock we fell out into formations, and names would be called. Those called had to report to go to Vietnam. I spent four days there. They were bad, just waiting for something to happen. On the fourth morning, my name was called. I went to a holding area where they issued jungle fatigues and clothing, and we had to put it all in a duffel bag.

We flew from California to Guam and Japan on the way to Vietnam. I arrived in Vietnam on June 23, 1968, which was just after the Tet Offensive began, but it was still going on. We flew into Binh Hoa, which is about twenty-five miles from Saigon, and went to the 90th Replacement Battalion. The first thing I remember seeing was when I looked out of the plane, which was making a bank to the right. I looked down and saw lights going in every direction. I told the soldier sitting next to me that it must be a big airport because it looked like a lot of planes were landing. But the lights weren't planes. The pilot announced that we were in a holding pattern because the airport was under attack. He said we would land as soon as they ran away the Viet Cong and repaired the runways. The lights were actually tracers. We landed about one o'clock in the morning, and as soon as we stepped off the plane the smell was terrible, kind of like an outdoor toilet. The heat was so bad that within a few seconds we were soaking with sweat, and the heat was like that the whole year we were over there. In what they call winter, it got down to the seventies or maybe eighties.

My MOS was that of a clerk during my basic training. When I got to Vietnam, I was assigned to MACV, which is Military Assistance Command Vietnam. I was on Advisory Team 118. I worked with scout dogs. My sergeant was Staff Sergeant Leisk, who had been in the 9th Infantry and the 25th Infantry. He had worked with the scout dogs with both. Scout dogs are used for reconnaissance. They are taught not to bark. They don't attack like sentry dogs do. We worked with the 1st Vietnamese Division, and our job was to go with them. We did have interpreters with us. Our job was to go out and check for enemy troop movements within about a twenty-five radius of Saigon. We didn't always work in that area, though, because sometimes they would bring in helicopters and transport us somewhere else, occasionally half a day away.

With what we did, we might be in jungles or rice paddies or whatever. If we saw any activity that we thought might indicate the enemy, we would report it. It was hard to tell because a lot of the people over there wore black pajamas. We called them pajamas, but they actually were pants and shirts. You may encounter the enemy at night, but during the day they might be in a village, cooking or something, like a regular citizen. Usually, though, if we observed anything out of the ordinary at night or lights that didn't belong in a certain area, then we reported that.

We went through a lot of villages. There again it was to report anything. The Vietnamese we worked with were the ones that mostly checked in the little huts and buildings to see if there was any ammunition or firearms or anything that shouldn't have been there. You could not tell the villagers from the enemy. You could tell the NVA, which is the North Vietnamese Army, because they had a beige-colored outfit. The Viet Cong, which were actually the South Vietnamese rebels, did not have uniforms.

The time we were out on a mission varied. If there were reports of enemy movements, we might be out five or six days. Usually, it was limited to two or three days. We would sleep wherever we could, even standing up against trees or sitting on their roots. We usually slept under our ponchos. We tried not to carry too much. We were usually more worried about having several extra pairs of socks along with extra food and ammunition and not worry too much about other things. We would wear our clothes five or six days. We might not have a bath for that long, and if we did, it was under a drum with a spigot and water heated by the sun.

The jungle wasn't always as you see it in the movies. There was a lot of small undergrowth that needed to be cut. If there were big trees, not as much undergrowth was present. Sometimes, though, you had to cut through with a machete to get even a couple hundred yards, and then you might hit an opening where you walked maybe a fourth of a mile. It was tough and it was hot. The humidity was so bad it felt like you couldn't take a deep breath without getting your lungs full of water. The monsoon season came a little bit after we arrived. We thought it was never going to quit raining. The rice paddies were fertilized with human waste, and they had a real bad smell, and even after you changed socks, the smell was still there. We did have leeches, but we kept our boots bloused, which helped some. If we got leeches, we used cigarettes to burn them off of each other.

We worked in the Mekong Delta, but not a lot. I had some buddies who worked the waterways down there with armored boats. Mostly, though, we worked in the rice paddies and jungles outside of Saigon.

If we spotted the enemy, we would not engage them unless it was a small group, like two or three. Most of the time, we were out-numbered because there would only be six or seven of us. In those cases, we would withdraw and report. Our air support was the 82nd Airborne. If we found any troops that we thought might make a movement into Saigon or move onto some of our troops, we called in air strikes or artillery or whatever we thought was needed. The 82nd also supplied us with helicopters. They would pick us up with our dogs and take us to whatever area we were going to, then drop us off and pick us up later.

A scout dog will actually warn you. You travel with your hand on his neck and throat. Of course, a dog has a lot better sense of smell than a human. The dogs could detect trip wires that set off the booby traps that the VC had all around in the jungle. They would growl if they detected the trip wires or troops or personnel of any kind except the ones they had been around. We depended on those dogs. We had certain ones we worked with, and the South Vietnamese had dogs they worked with. We worked mainly out of the Military Dog Training Center, which was about halfway between Binh Hoa and Saigon. I think there was also another group that handled dogs in the southern area below Saigon.

If we spotted VC, we reported it to the 82nd. We also had to inform them about troop movements and what action we had taken. If there were big troop movements, we called it in and they would order air strikes. That is how it usually wound up.

We were busy. They would tell us the area we needed to go to. We went all around, even up as far north as Pleiku. The area near the junction between Laos and Cambodia was called the "three corners area". When President Johnson made a report to the nation and said we had no troops in those two countries, we were probably twenty-five or thirty miles into Cambodia. We were looking for troop movements up in that area because the enemy would come down from Laos into Cambodia on their way to Vietnam. Spies were also coming in.

Most of the firefights we had were in the jungles. A lot of the fire was blind. What you would do was look for the yellow muzzle flashes, leaf movements, or anything out of the ordinary and fire at it if you saw it. It was usually pretty close range. If we found where we thought supplies were coming through, we would usually mine it and call for an air strike. The Ho Chin Minh trail, which was a main supply route, was in our area.

In between missions, we would usually go to Saigon to make our reports to MACV headquarters and tell them what we had done, what we had found, and what we had accomplished.

We didn't encounter that many tunnels. We found a few, and when we did we'd just throw a hand grenade in. We didn't go in, but we would blow it up if we found an entrance.

The first weapon I was given was a Thompson .45 which shot a .45 automatic round. Of course, one of the bad things about it was that you could go through a clip in just no time. Within three weeks or a month, we were issued an M-16. We kept our weapon as clean as we could out where we were. A lot of guys had trouble with them jamming with mud and everything. I did fire at the enemy, and I'm sure that I must have killed some. It's hard to tell, though, because they were frequently in the bushes or jungle and we couldn't see them. After I got back, I did feel guilty and talked to my preacher. His reply was that we were under orders and that one of our jobs was to stay alive, and that made me feel a lot better about things that had happened over there. What I was doing was a long way from being a typist.

I was over there for a year. They called it Tour 365. You got a day of travel going over and a day of travel coming back, so I guess it should have been called Tour 363. The Army has what they called OJT, or on the job training. If you are not trained for a job, you will be put with someone who is. I spent about a month with Sergeant Leisk, training to be doing what we would be doing. Other than that month, I spent the rest of my tour doing the missions.

I have hunted all my life and was used to weapons. As a matter of fact, I was on the rifle team at Florence State, so I felt pretty comfortable with the weapons. But that didn't keep me from being scared the whole time I was over there. They say in the military you never hear the round that kills you. I was fired on at least weekly, but the good thing was that I heard all of them, and never was injured, either. We lost some of the scout dogs, and one of the Vietnamese with us got blown up by a booby trap. I don't know if he didn't hear the dog growl or whatever. But he got in the booby trap, and it also killed two guys who worked with us. I was there when it happened and saw it.

Like I said, our job was to go through villages. I guess one of the worst things was one time when we went into one of these villages. I had a friend who was in ROTC when I was at Florence State. In the village we found that US soldiers had engaged the enemy because we found some bodies of our soldiers. If the bodies had been there a day or two, they had swelled to a humongous size, and these had. We called it in and the bodies were picked up. A week later, I saw in the "Stars and Stripes" that my friend from college was one of the soldiers killed there.

There were usually five or six in our group when we went out. Sometimes, though, we would split up with three going one way and three another to be able to cover a larger area. We never knew what we might encounter in the jungle. It is sort of like driving in Atlanta. You are on guard constantly. You are tensed up and looking everywhere for something that is out of place, a limb moving that shouldn't be, keeping aware of trip wires and booby traps. The VC would dig a hole in the middle of a trail. They would sharpen bamboo and heat treat it, then put human waste on the end. This was done to cause infections. If going in the pit didn't kill you, then the infection would or at least take you out of action.

The dogs did give us a little bit more sense of security. You learn to depend on them. The infantry had what was called point men. We didn't have one, so we took turns walking out front, and this person was usually the first to receive fire.

We got most of our supplies from the 82nd Airborne, like ammunition and all. We had C-rations which had been packed up for the Korean war, and that is what we ate a lot of. We carried rice with us, which is one reason I don't eat rice today.

I went in as a PFC. Like I said, the guy I worked with was Staff

Sergeant Leisk. He had been all the way up to E-8. I guess he had had some problems because he was an E-6 then. I had a Vietnamese lieutenant that spoke pretty good English and was the interpreter, so he may have actually been in charge. I worked real close with him. There would usually be six or eight Vietnamese with us, and a couple of them would have dogs too.

Our breaks depended on what our headquarters wanted. Sometimes we would come and stay for a full day or we might just stay for a few hours. We'd get some different clothes, re-supply our ammunition, and go on the road again.

For a long time we had trouble with the Vietnamese soldiers with us. We depended on them. If you are trying to sleep when you have been on patrol for twelve or fourteen hours, you are completely bushed and need a nap. You depend on whoever is watching wherever you are lying down for security. When we depended on the Vietnamese, a lot of the time they would be gone or asleep. They would just take off and go. I harbored a real resentment for a long time about them doing us that way. It was almost like you were not allowed to sleep. You had to always keep an eye on what was going on to see if the enemy was coming into your camp. Our lives depended on that, and they just didn't seem to care.

When I was over there, we had guys in supply, infantry, artillery, helicopter pilots and all that we dealt with. The jets would give us support. We could call "red ball" which was the 82nd Airborne base camp. There were all kinds of names for different landing zones and things. If we called "red ball", they would have air support for us in a short time. I don't think it ever took over fifteen minutes. It must have been a deal MACV had worked out with the 82nd.

Our base camp was a place called Govap, which was about fifteen miles out of Saigon toward Binh Hoa. If we were going on a mission a long ways away, they would fly us out of Long Binh or Saigon in cargo planes. There were airfields way up South Vietnam at Pleiku and Kon Tum where we would go. When we got there, they would helicopter us to wherever we were going on our mission. But we stayed mostly in the general area of our base camp.

I had one week of R&R time when they flew me to Hawaii. When we went to Saigon, we usually had Vietnamese drivers who had Jeeps, and they took us in to make our reports. Saigon at that time was a busy place. We went there once in a while for relaxation but didn't get into any major trouble. However, we might get into a fight with Marines or something like that.

The troops I was with didn't have any problems with drugs. Of course, they may have a little pot or something. Heroin over there was easy to get, and a lot of older Vietnamese smoked it, but we didn't. I always wanted to keep my mind where it would be sharp. I know that Sergeant Leisk did, too. We knew our lives depended on our being able to think clearly. I think a lot of these drug problems you see in movies are drawn out of proportion. The drug problems that some of them had may have been related to all the Agent Orange that was sprayed, which defoliated a lot of the country. I do know that a lot of the Vietnamese troops with us did use the drugs, but the American troops didn't nearly as much, around us anyway.

We left Vietnam on June 23rd, exactly a year after we had been flown in. We flew nonstop to Oakland, where we got new clothing. We had come in out of the field with dirty clothes and mud on our boots. They gave us a shower, gave us our new clothing, and gave us a steak. I went on leave for thirty days, then to Fort Stewart, Georgia, for the rest of my time, which was as a game warden at Fort Stewart, Georgia. I thought they had dogs I would work with, but they didn't. The Fort had about 286,000 acres, which was nothing much but woods. I had been out in the woods hunting and fishing most of my life, and I was happy there. I got out on January 23, 1970.

We were told not to wear our military uniforms on the way home because of all the opposition to the war. I think the troops from WWII and Korea had been able to wear their uniforms when they got home. When we were in Vietnam, we had read a little bit about the opposition to the war, but we didn't know it was as bad as it was. I didn't have any problems, but a lot of the guys I've talked to since then had been spat on and called a "baby killer". I'm sure there were times when babies were killed if the troops had orders to go in and wipe out a village. Our superiors never gave us any orders like that. They let us use our own discretion. I know of one case when we were in Saigon when a woman had put a hand grenade under a baby. The grenade went off and killed two soldiers who were going by. Like the Taliban now, they used any method they could to kill or injure.

I returned home and worked at several places. I tried to get on at TVA for two or three years. They were supposed to take veterans first, but in 1973, I finally went to work there. I am concerned that companies then and now do not give veterans preference. I was a machinist at first, then worked as a boilermaker for the last twenty years or so. I am retired from TVA.

In the military, I was making ninety dollars a month, but in Vietnam I got an extra sixty-five dollars in hazardous duty pay, which wasn't much to risk your life for. We were over there to do a mission, and it probably wouldn't have mattered if they paid us more or less, we would have done the same thing as well as we could. We had been taught that. I have been up to Washington twice and have seen friends of mine I worked with on that wall but not any from my group.

I think the Vietnam war was very stressful. You were looking out all the time. They had snipers, just like we did. You might be going through an area and get sniper fire, but that happened only once to us. A Vietnamese soldier was injured. But you never knew who was there in the dense jungle.

I have been really active in the VFW and the American Legion. I had always heard they were places people went to drink, so I didn't join the VFW until the nineties when I found out the post here didn't have any drinking and had community activities. I made myself a promise that guys who came from the military weren't going to be treated like those from Vietnam. They were going to be welcomed home. We have a riders group at our post, and we provide escorts. When the local guard unit came back, we met them over at Fort Payne and escorted them back on motorcycles. They turned out from school at Plainview in Rainsville, and those kids waved American flags. This really gets to you when you see something like that, compared to what we came home to. We give them gifts and feed them a dinner. We send care packages to those overseas.

I've thought a lot about whether the war was worth it. What we went over there initially for was to stop communism, and that was the right thing to do. I think the way our politicians handled it was not necessarily right. We lost over 58,000 soldiers. There were times when we went out when we could not even load our weapons. Of course, they stopped using napalm on the Viet Cong and NVA, saying it was inhumane. But they didn't see what the Viet Cong and NVA did to our troops they captured. I think that if the politicians had gotten a little taste of that, they wouldn't have been so quick to stop the napalm, which was one thing the enemy really feared. It was horrible, and that is why they stopped it. If a person dies, it doesn't matter if he was burned to death or hit with a bullet. Either way, he dies. Any war you have, civilians will be killed, children, women and men. If you go into war, you need to go into it to win in order to stop whatever action you went in to stop. We had things that weren't used over there. Also, a lot of money was made in that war. Every piece of mail we shipped was mailed for free, but every piece of mail that came in had an emblem of two bluebirds. I often wondered if this stood for Lady Bird Johnson's contracting firm.

Dennis Miller

Dennis Miller was a member of a "sweep and clear" team in Vietnam. Its mission was to go into the villages and surrounding rugged areas by foot and make contact with the enemy. As a consequence, the unit often encountered the enemy and was involved in frequent firefights. Dennis considers himself fortunate not to have been seriously injured, but he did witness his buddies getting shot or killed.

My name is Dennis Wayne Miller. I was born on December 24, 1945, in Gatesville, Texas, but grew up in west Texas in the Lubbock area. I joined the Army at seventeen and went to Fort Polk, Louisiana, for basic training and also advanced infantry training. From there, I went to Fort Benning, Georgia, for jump school. After I completed jump school, I was assigned to the 101st Airborne Division in Fort Campbell, Kentucky. I stayed there until January 1966, when I was deployed to Vietnam. I had turned twenty in December, and in January I was in Vietnam. I left from Oakland. They told us we wouldn't need our winter uniforms over there, so they packed mine away in two boxes. They told me they would send them to my house after I returned.

We arrived in Saigon and put in at a replacement center for a couple of days. Then we went to the Airborne base camp in Nha Trang. At that time, there was no permanent housing, and the runway was made of steel grates. We were temporarily in tents. We weren't there long at all. I got assigned to my unit, the 327th Infantry Battalion.

Our mission was to go on what was called "sweep and clear" operations. We would helicopter into an area, and after landing, we would have objectives for which we would march through rice paddies, mountains, and jungles. Our mission was to go into these villages and areas and make contact with the enemy if we could. Basically, it was an intelligence-finding operation. As I said, we went through these areas by foot, and often we would encounter the enemy.

We would get C-rations and mail every three or four days by helicopter. The uniform was jungle fatigues, and it seemed like it was difficult to get replacements. Myself and several others had trousers that were just worn out and all ripped. The climate was so hot that many of us didn't wear underwear. The boxer-type underwear would tear and get tangled up, and the brief kind would get too binding and hot, so we might not wear either. One time my trousers tore from the crotch to the knee, and after two or three days, they were torn all the way down the leg. One thing I'll never forget, among other things, was it seemed like every bush in Vietnam had thorns, and if it didn't have thorns, it had ants that would take a plug out of you. That was just an every-day happening.

On these missions, we would start with a company of men. We would set up in various areas. Sometimes we would go single file through the area and other times we would go "on line", which means spread out. Most of the time, particularly in the jungles and mountains, we were in two columns. We might be out a week or so. Sometimes they would pick us up and take us back to a secure place for as long as two days to rest up, then we would be picked up, taken to some area, and begin a new mission. That was the routine. The heat didn't bother me all that much because I was young, but the torrential rains were aggravating. All you had was a poncho and what you were wearing. We didn't have tents, just the poncho, so we slept on the ground.

Mosquitoes were real heavy, but we took malaria tablets daily. In the rice paddies and river crossings we had to contend with leeches. We would have to stop and pick them off. We carried three or four days rations on our back along with ample ammunition. The only time we bathed was when we were near a creek or river. Most of us didn't shave but every third or fourth day. We just didn't stay anywhere very long; we just picked up and moved. Movies like "Platoon" were pretty accurate in showing the conditions of how it was over there.

We encountered the enemy more than I wanted to. I remember shortly after I got there I was involved in my first encounter. We were in two columns, single-file, going through a jungle. In this kind of formation, we could be ten yards apart or as far as thirty-five yards. Thirty or so men would be in each column. We started receiving fire. I didn't realize it, but when a bullet comes close to you, you don't hear a crack or ricochet like you hear on the TV. It is a loud snap or pop kind of sound. I can't describe it, but I guess that is the bullet breaking the air. We were in columns, and one of the enemy came out of a hole in the ground and took off running away from us. It put me in mind like when I was a boy in West Texas and went jack rabbit hunting with a semi-automatic .22 rifle. You fire to see where the rounds hit behind the rabbit until you reach it. That is the way it was with the Vietnamese man running. A couple of us fired on him and brought him down. That was my first encounter and was early on.

US troops weren't the only ones over there fighting the VC. I remember one time we were on a mission, and we went by helicopter to a cemetery that was surrounded by rice paddies. About 150 to 200 yards away was a tree-lined little village. Korean troops were at the cemetery. We came in to relieve them. One of them told me there were many VC. I looked around and could see shell casings scattered around, which meant there had been some action about. The Koreans moved out the same day. We were there a couple of days without any action. At night we would send fire teams of three men out to set up claymore land mines. These are packets of explosives in the shape of a U. They are steel balls compressed into C-4. You face the outer portion toward the enemy and then you run trip wires to set it off. We had gone out there for two or three nights on the outpost, as it was called, in front of the rest of the company to set up the mines. Three men were in each position, and each position was about thirty yards apart.

Then one day our 2nd lieutenant from New Mexico got the bright idea that we needed to shave, and we didn't have any shaving water. Outside of this village was a mud/brick house with a thatched roof and a short mud fence around it. It was maybe thirty or forty yards outside the main part of the village. Somebody said that was where the head of the village lived, but I don't know. This lieutenant ordered our sergeant to go up to this place where he knew there would be a well and bring back shaving water for the guys in the camp. There were six of us who went. The sergeant was a black fellow named Redding. There was a guy from Philadelphia named Downey, one from Ohio named Bushengberg, the radio man Roland from Arkansas, a guy named Elisovsky, and me.

We got five-gallon gas cans and left the rest of the company. We walked along rice paddy dikes that were about twelve to fifteen inches high and just wide enough to walk on. We went around the front of the house to a gate. I set my rifle against the entrance of the gate and squatted down, scanning the line of the village with binoculars. You could see trees and structures about fifty yards off. One of the guys climbed up a coconut tree and brought some coconuts down. We drank the milk but didn't eat the meat. At that time I was a smoker, and the only cigarettes we had were in C-rations and were mostly Camels and unfiltered Pall Malls. Occasionally you would get a Winston, a Salem, or something else. One of the guys had Marlboros, which we called A-Class. We were by the well where we were filling the cans, and he passed around these filtered cigarettes. We got the cans full and started back, walking three or four yards apart single-file on the rice paddy dikes.

We got about twenty yards past the wall at the residence and started getting heavy rifle fire. Of course, the first thing we did was hit the water beside the dike for cover. Looking toward the village, I never saw a person but I could see movement in the bushes and where the rifle fire was coming from. We returned fire as best as we could. Roland, the radioman, was shot in the head and was killed. Elisovsky was also shot in the head and killed. Sergeant Redding got shot. The bullet went through his canteen and into his back. He went to Roland's radio and called for assistance. It seemed forever, but our company did come through the paddies in force. At that time we carried M-16s with twenty rounds but had forty rounds available. Of course, we carried magazines in our ammo pouches and boxed ammo in our backpack. I can't tell you exactly what I did, but I know I emptied two magazine rounds. I was in the rice paddy during this time, lying on my belly and shooting. The water was jumping up from the rounds coming at you.

So our company was coming toward us and the enemy was in the tree line in the village, and we were in between. Some members of the company were wounded coming to get us. The company moved on past us toward the village Then the Medical Evacuation helicopters flew in and we loaded the ones who had been shot. Some of the bravest men I saw over there were those pilots and their gunners.

Anyway, we got back to the graveyard where we had our positions. An air strike was ordered, and they bombed the hell out of that village with napalm and other bombs. They came in and debriefed us the best they could, but I remember just lying there with my breathing so heavy I thought I was going to go out of this world. Of course, I was terrified, but I was angry over all of that just for shaving water.

There is more to this incident. Either late that night or the next night we went back into that village in-force on a reconnaissance mission. I don't know why they didn't want us to engage. In those villages, they have certain areas set aside for gardens. It was real quiet when we went into the village. We hunkered down in a garden, looking for movement. I could see enemy troops coming down the walkways of the villages. You could see their rifles glistening in the moonlight. We were maybe ten or fifteen yards from them as they came through. I thought we would jump up and start firing on them any minute, but the commander decided we would lay low. So they went on by but didn't see us. We spent most of that night in that village and snuck out before daylight. Here I was, an E-4 specialist rifleman; so you know that I didn't know what the commander was trying to do.

(Note: Several weeks after our interview, Dennis obtained internet research concerning Elisovsky. David Henry Elisovsky was a sergeant in the Army from Cordova, Arkansas. He was born on 7/24/1947 and killed in action on 1/23/1966. Dennis says that actually seeing those dates made the intervening forty-six years seem to melt away, bringing back the immediacy and horror of the battle in which those comrades were killed.)

That was the last of the activity there. We went back to a mountain top for two days for rest, then we did the same thing all over again. We would be picked up by the helicopters and taken to another village. I don't know what the average age was of the soldier on the ground, but I would think it may have been between nineteen and twenty-five. We were all nervous and jumpy.

The first men in the columns as we went single-file might be members of the fire team, but sometimes we would alternate. Often times I would be on point as the first man, and that is a scary deal. The Vietnamese were notorious for booby traps like stakes of sharpened bamboo with human waste on the tips to cause infections. They also used booby trap hand grenades with a trip wire, as well as landmines. One man could be responsible for killing the soldiers behind him if he set off one of those traps as he went through, but this couldn't be helped. We did not have specially trained dogs that could detect the traps. We traveled with a Vietnamese interpreter.

One time we were traveling through the jungle, and we had heard there was a training camp in this remote area. At least, that was the intelligence. We were in two columns going up this mountain. We always carried our weapons on automatic, ready to fire. Well, we received fire, and everybody hit the ground and tried to figure out where the firing was coming from. We had an M-79 grenade launcher, which is much like a single-shot shotgun, that breaks down and has a projectile with a five meter killing radius. Our sergeant, who was from Hawaii, determined where the fire was coming from. He got the M-79 and fired about four rounds in that direction. The enemy's rifle fire stopped, and we advanced on. When we got to our destination, it was a training camp. They had dug ditches just narrow enough to walk in. We found one dead enemy in a ditch, and it looked like he took a direct hit from one those M-79 rounds. I jumped in the ditch and saw he had full US military gear on. Most of it was shredded, but I took my knife and cut the rest of the threads and took it up out of there. He had American hand grenades so new the paint wasn't even scratched. That is when I first heard about the black market in Vietnam. They were buying US materials from somebody. Here again, they took us out for a couple days rest, and then we would go out again.

The going out like this was all the time. My feet stayed wet. We had extra socks that we would tie onto our gear to try to dry, but you couldn't keep them dry. My feet stayed wet so long that I got what they call "jungle rot" in my toes, and they got infected. I was sent to a hospital in Nha Trang and stayed four or five days. Another time I developed dengue fever, which is kind of like malaria. My fever was actually so high that they packed me in ice. I was in the 85th Evacuation

Hospital. I believe it was in Nha Trang. Then I went back to the company. Again, it was so much more of the same; helicopter into an area, unload, do the mission, then come back.

We could recognize the enemy only if they had a gun and were shooting at us. I saw innocent people die in different ways. Once we were clearing a village, going door-to-door checking these little huts made of grass and mud and sticks. Some of us were on the left of this little street and the others were on the opposite side. I heard fire when they went into a hut. I went over there. In the hut was a prayer corner where they go to pray. Something like a banner was hanging on the wall all the way to the floor. An old man, who no doubt had gotten scared himself, had hidden behind this banner. When the troops had entered the hut, they saw movement behind the banner and cut him down. The man who shot him almost went crazy. It really worked on him, and you could see why.

I had a Starlight scope. This thing was about two feet long and was carried in a case. It's not exactly like a camera. It picks up images with the moonlight or starlight or any light at all, so you see images at night. Once we were on just another mission and had been told to gather intelligence. One night six of us went out and found several of the enemy around a campfire. Looking through this scope, I could see maybe four or five figures. I knew they were the enemy because I could see their rifles and other gear. Our sergeant decided we would engage and then get the hell out of there. Each of us was told to fire one magazine, so we sighted in on this group and fired one magazine each and hauled ourselves out of there. The next day we went in there and found a lot of blood but no bodies. They obviously took the bodies with them.

There are so many incidents that come back as I talk. It didn't take me long after I got to Vietnam for me to tell myself that if I didn't get hit in the head or in the main portion of my body, I was getting out of there and going home. I was a soldier and I followed orders, but I also had a mind of my own. If I didn't think it was the thing to do, I just said "yes sir" and did what I wanted to do. You have to look after yourself. I was only twenty years old and just marked my days off on the calendar. I had a date that I was going to leave. I don't know how many missions I was on. We would have our rest periods, then do the "search and clear" and intelligence missions in the mountains, rice paddies, and jungles.

We never worked side-by-side with the South Vietnamese army. I didn't have much contact with them at all. As far as a uniformed enemy is concerned, we only encountered them once. I guess we were near Cambodia and came upon what we called hard-core troops that were uniformed, and we got into a fight with them. I was just an enlisted man and not in the know about what all we accomplished after this encounter, but I do know there were two or three of them dead. One of them had a big satchel like a briefcase that had a lot of papers in it. I hope they were of some use. We also captured a cache of dozens and dozens of rifles and munitions in a cave area.

Here is another thing; when Americans took prisoners, in my opinion they were treated humanely. A helicopter would come get them and take them off somewhere. For instance, one time we were stranded on the side of a mountain. Two fire teams had been told to find an easier way to get down the mountain. We started off in two groups of six. We had been walking through this big jungle area on the mountain for about two hours. I was the point man and came up on this enormous spider in a web. It was beautiful, so I stopped everybody and called them to come look at it. This spider probably saved all our lives, because we hadn't realized we were about to meet some Viet Cong coming up the mountain, just yards away. We could see them in the brush after we had stopped. The standard rule is to engage and get the heck out of there. So we all engaged and then hot-footed it back the way we came to the company. Some more of the company went back to the same location, and we found one Viet Cong who was alive but had been shot in the hip a couple of times. We carried him out of there, and a helicopter flew in to take him for medical treatment.

The only injury I got was white phosphorus grenade burns, but they were from our own grenades. At night, our artillery would send up flares out in front of us to see if there was any movement. When the flare would explode, the big canister it was fired in would fall to the ground. You could hear them at night. They made a whooshing sound as air passed through them, and then you would hear them when they hit the ground, and you hoped it didn't fall on you. There was a bird over there that made a similar whooshing sound. We had an encounter one night when some of the white phosphorus grenades were thrown. One landed near me and burned me a little bit. Actually, I was very fortunate.

One day I was carrying the Starlight scope. We were crossing over a big rice paddy at the base of a mountain. I was point man. We were headed to the tree line and started getting fire. Bullets were landing all around us in the water, in front of us, and behind us. I turned around so fast that scope swung around and knocked my helmet off. This is the weirdest thing and I will never forget it. I probably wasn't twenty yards from the dike that was the only cover. When that scope knocked that helmet off, I was running as fast as I could through the water to get to the dike. It was just like a dream, because I felt I was running in slow motion. I just couldn't run fast enough, and it seemed so slow. I could see the water popping up from the bullets. I know I got there quick, but it didn't seem like it. I dove over that dike. Of course, I couldn't see the enemy. An air strike was called. You know, war is not pretty, but it was pretty to see those jets come in and napalm the side of that mountain. Napalm is just liquid fire. When the jets drop that barrel of napalm, it hits and explodes into fire. It is quite effective.

I could tell about all kinds of incidents because there was one all the time. The military needs youths as ground soldiers because of their energy and determination. Also, after they are trained, they will follow orders. That is what that age group does. There is a certain amount of pride in having the ability and knowledge to do the job you are trained for. When I first got there, all of us were really scared because we didn't know what to expect. After a while, I guess I did get hardened to it. I could wrap up in my poncho and sleep three or four hours at a time. The new guys would stay up all night with their rifle in their hands. You do get accustomed to sleeping and resting when you can. You never really lose your fear but you do get used to it, or at least you don't fear as much unless there is a need for it.

There wasn't all the news media there is today. The only thing we had was an occasional "Stars and Stripes" paper. I didn't hear much over there about Jane Fonda and people like her, but I don't respect her. I didn't know what to expect when I came home. We were told when we left Vietnam that our baggage and us would be searched when getting on the plane and when getting off. As I said, I didn't have anything. My clothes were about worn out and my duffel bags that I left at base camp were scattered and gone when I got back there. I couldn't even get a Class-A uniform at the base camp, so I had to buy an Air Force uniform to put my Army brass on. All I had was a little bag they call an AWOL bag, like a tote bag, with my shaving gear and my underclothes in it. I did have a bayonet in my boot. There were no metal detectors and I was never searched. I got on that plane with that bayonet and still had it in my boot when I got off in California. I didn't know what to expect. By then, I had heard that they were spitting on veterans and throwing rocks at them when they came back. I didn't have any problems like that.

The Vietnamese had hand hair clippers, and everybody wore their hair just as close as they could get it. Of course, there were always a few hairs around your ears and low spots and missed spots. I went to a barber shop in Garland, Texas, when I got out to get my first civilian haircut. The barber wanted to know who in the world had been cutting my hair. I told him, and he gave me a haircut free.

The tour in Vietnam was for a year, but I was only over there for six months. My enlisted time served ended and I was brought home. After what I went through over there, I think there was a plan for me or I wouldn't be here talking to you. I came so close so many times to dying, and people around me did die. You wonder why I was the lucky one. I was a part of killing. I don't know how many.

In Vietnam, I got service medals for different campaigns and the Combat Infantryman's Badge, which is given by units once they engage the enemy. Coming back in one piece was enough for me.

After I got out, I moved to Fort Worth and went to work for General Dynamics for over four years. Then I bumped around for a while, doing a couple of jobs. Then I moved to Zeleinople, Pennsylvania, to work in a copper mill for Halstead Mitchell. They built a plant here in Scottsboro, and we came here late in 1973. Once I got here, I decided I would rather be a policeman, so I went to work for the Scottsboro Police Department for seventeen years. Then I went to the sheriff's office in December 1990 and retired last year as the sheriff.

At this point, all I can say in general about the war in Vietnam is that I don't feel it was worth the cost.

I'm still waiting on the two boxes of winter uniforms they packed away when I left Oakland to go to Vietnam.

Wally Haralson

Judge Wally Haralson is a bona fide and proud veteran of the Vietnam War, yet has never been in Vietnam. From a base in Thailand, he flew tankers that refueled fighters on bombing missions to Hanoi, Haiphong, and other targets. Wally estimates that he averaged over thirty refueling missions each month.

My name is William Wallace Haralson. I was born in Gadsden, Alabama, on 18 April 1939. We lived in Fort Payne, but there was no hospital in town. I was raised in Fort Payne and went to Dekalb County High School for two years, then graduated from McCallie School in Chattanooga.

After high school, I spent two years at Marion Military Institute looking towards an Air Force career. I spent two-and-a-half years at the Air Force Academy, then transferred to the University of Alabama. While at the University, I was the commander of the Air Force ROTC unit, which made me eligible for a regular commission in the Air Force. As a prospective career officer, it is important to have a regular commission as opposed to a reserve commission. While there, I learned to fly through the flight instructor program in the ROTC. I flew a Cessna 172 and was able to get a private pilot's license while I was at the university.

I graduated from Alabama in January of 1963. My pilot training date was not until the following September, so I had several months to kill before I went into the Air Force. I went back to Fort Payne and taught ninth grade English at Dekalb County High School. I spent the summer as a lifeguard; then my career started for real.

In September of 1963 I went to Craig Air Force Base in Selma for a one-year pilot training program where we flew jets. Pilot training was divided into six month parts, as it still is today. The first six months is primary, and basic is the second six months. In the first six months, I flew T-37s, which were little two-seaters. In the last six months, I flew T-33s. In September of 1964 I got my wings, which means I successfully completed my training in a one-year course.

I was assigned to the Strategic Air Command (SAC) as a co-pilot on KC-135s, which are re-fueling aircraft, and are essentially Boeing 707s. It was a four-engine jet tanker. I went to Castle Air Force Base in California. I actually had one more month left out there when the Pueblo crisis hit, and they needed all the tankers that were in any kind of use. I remember my instructor told me we had been taught all they could any way, so we might just as well go to our next assignment. I had gotten married during my training period, so my new wife and I drove from Merced, California, to Columbus, Ohio. We took six days, and that was the nearest we came to a honeymoon.

I set up shop as a KC-135 co-pilot in the 301st Refueling Wing at Lockbourne Air Force Base in Columbus. Our duty was threefold. One of these was that we were assigned to the SAC and were part of the long-range bombing concept which had to do with the cold war. While at Lockbourne, we were assigned to a bomber wing in upstate New York. The mission, should it have ever happened, was that if there were a nuclear war, we would take off from Lockbourne and fly to the southern tip of Greenland. Our B-47 bombers would take off from upstate New York, and we would refuel them over Greenland. The bombers' mission was to go on and bomb Russia and then head for the Middle East. There was no other place they could go, and they would basically crash land somewhere there if they got that far. Our mission, oddly enough, was to land at Thule Air Force Base in Greenland, refuel, and come home. The problem was that in the event of war, there would not be a Thule because it would have been targeted by the Russians and would just be a big cinder.

Our crew decided if that did happen and that after we had refueled the bombers, the best we could hope for was to turn around and head to northern Canada since we wouldn't be able to make it back to the base. We decided it might be best to land on a snow field or ice cap, which would be better than bailing out, which was like a Chinese fire drill to do. To bail out, a boom operator had to pull down a handle from the side of the plane, which would blow a door off. Then a grate had to be lifted up that hung over the hole made when the bar was lowered. Next you hung from the bar and dropped from the bottom of the plane. All that just didn't seem like a good idea at the time. So we all decided we would try bellying it in, not that our chances of survival were very good, but at least we would all be together. The next decision would have been whether to leave the wheels up, and we never did decide that one.

Another part of our mission was to pull alert duty at Goose Bay Air Force Base in Labrador. We shared the base with the old Vulcan bomber that the Brits had. This bomber was in one of the 007 movies and was a bat-wing plane. We spent many a night at the officers club drinking Shirley Temples, which were just pink lemonade. We were on alert and couldn't drink alcohol.

The third part of our mission was the longest part. We took off from Lockbourne and flew to March Air Force Base in Riverside, California, and spent the night. The next day, loaded with fuel, we would rendezvous with fighters, usually F-4 Phantoms, and escort them to Honolulu, refueling them a couple of times along the way. We would land at Hickam Field in Honolulu. By then we would have a good idea of who the fighter pilots were and would make arrangements to meet at the officers club to have a drink and dinner and see them for the first time face-to-face. On one occasion we saw Bob Newhart when he was just an up-and-coming comedian.

The next morning we got up early and headed for Guam, which was a nine-hour flight. The fighters would take off later and catch up with us to be refueled three times during the flight. We landed at Anderson Air Force Base in Guam. Usually about thirty B-52 bombers were stationed there at any time, and that was the stopping place for bomb runs over Hanoi, Haiphong, and other targets. It was a twelve-hour flight for the bombers to take off from Guam, perform their mission, and get back to Guam. So we had what was called strip alert duty. About an hour before the first bombers were due back, which was usually two or three in the morning, we cranked our tanker up and taxied out to the end of the runway. We sat on one side of the runway with the number four engine idling with the others shut down. With the 135, you always started the other engines off of number four. Thankfully we never had to do it, but our mission would have been that if a tanker had trapped fuel or had some fuel they could not use, we would have gone out and refueled them. It did happen several times, but I never was called up to do it. Often, the pilot and other two crew members would go in the back leaving me, the co-pilot, sitting in front. It was kind of surreal because you sat out there maybe an hour-and-a-half and watched the bombers come in. So that is what we did the two or three days on Guam. I was a co-pilot the first three years but had my own crew the last year I was in SAC, which is about normal. The fighters we were with had already gone over to fighter bases like Ubon, Takli or Udorn in northern Thailand. A new bunch of fighters had come in, so we carried them with us from Guam, and they would peel away from us in Thailand and go to the fighter bases.

We went to Sattahip, which was our air base 150 miles below Bangkok on the Gulf of Siam. It was basically a special base built just for tankers. We were there thirty days and flew almost every day, sometimes twice a day. The missions were all the same but the rendezvous point would be different. We would take off from Sattahip and go to what was called the "race track" over Laos. The "race track" was an oval like a car race track, and the planes circled the "race track" at the same altitude. The fighters knew where we were, and our navigator would get them with us. The K-35 had several radio systems, so before the fighters left we could find what was called their strike frequency, which was the frequency they would talk on with each other. It was some of the damnedest chatter you ever heard. These guys were going in bombing Hanoi, bombing Haiphong, bombing industrial sites, bombing railroad sites, bombing whatever. Of course, they were dodging flak and missiles. A typical communication would be "We have a SAM, break left" or "Watch out for that anti-aircraft fire at the six position" or "I have a secondary", which meant what they had bombed had a huge explosion and fireball. I'll have to say we did lose a good many planes over North Vietnam, but our group didn't lose any. We had four fighters at a time, and it was just the luck of the draw that we didn't. However, when they returned they would be sucking fuel because they spent most of the bomb runs in after-burner, which is a souped-up part that makes them go faster but uses more fuel. So when they refueled, one guy would hook up and get just a little, then the next one, etc. Once they got enough to not flame out, they hooked up again and got pretty much a full load so they could go back to their base.

Our tanker had a tube that came down out of the back. Our boom operator would lie down in the back of the plane and drop it down. Then the fighter pilots would fly in and make contact with the boom. The boom was a long metal tube about twenty-five feet long that was stored under the plane when we weren't using it, and it would be at a forty-five degree angle for the refueling operation. The fighter plane would tuck in under our rear end. Normally, we went about 350 knots during the refueling.

Actually, the process looked a lot easier than it was. The fighter pilots were very good at formation flying. They were flying what they called an envelope, which was a cubic measure maybe six feet on each side. Once they were in that formation with the tanker, they could just fly in that formation to be refueled. The boom had something like a stinger in the middle of it. This was a second tube that came out of the main tube with a hose connector, and these would be stuck in to pass the fuel. The operator of the boom knew exactly how to place the boom. In fact, he would talk the fighters to the position he wanted them. When they got close, he would say something like "up six" or "up four" or whatever. When he said "hold it", that meant he wanted them to stay right there. He could move it around a little bit, though.

Our tanker held roughly110,000 pounds of fuel. A gallon of fuel weighs about seven pounds, so that would be almost 16,000 gallons. I don't remember how much the fighters held, but it was enough to go on the mission and then get back to refuel one more time.

Our crew consisted of four people. There was a pilot, who was the aircraft commander, along with a co-pilot, a navigator, and the boom operator. The boom operator was an enlisted man and always at least a sergeant. He was the key to the whole thing, more so than any of us.

We had about twenty tankers at the base and might have twelve to fifteen in the air at any one time. We did not fly in formation but we were in close proximity. Even with this many tankers, we never had a serious problem to arise in the refueling. Everybody was so good in what they were doing, we never had a single time when the fighter almost ran into us or something like that. There is one story a tanker pilot in another unit told me that was serious. One time, after a fighter had gotten attached to his tanker, it flamed out trying to get fuel. It ran out of gas, and the engine just shut down. The other fighter pilots said they could make it to the base on the fuel they had. So the tanker asked the pilot of the flamed-out plane what angle of dive he needed to keep his hydraulic system active. In other words, what speed would keep the turbine turning, which runs all the systems. The pilot indicated he needed 175 knots, so they both glided down. The tanker managed to hook up with the F-105 and get him some fuel. He got an air start on his engine and headed back to his base. The SAC wanted to court-martial the tanker pilot for putting his crew at risk. The Tactical Air Command wanted to give him a Medal of Honor. I think it was a wash and nothing ever came of it.

We had a few night missions, and I have seen those carpet bombs just walk through the jungles. We never heard them since we were flying so high on those missions, but you could see them. They were dropping 500 pound bombs in a straight line This was in the northern part of South Vietnam. We didn't fly over North Vietnam. However, we did fly over the Gulf of Tonkin, which was one of our refueling tracks. The Gulf was just swarming with Navy aircraft, for they did a lot of bombing, too, off of naval carriers in the Gulf. The closest I ever came to being in danger was in that area. A SAM, or surface-to-air missile, had missed a plane but was still going. It looked like a big telephone pole, which is how they are described. It was flying in an arc, and it arced in front of our plane maybe a quarter-of-a-mile away, then exploded a quarter-of-a-mile to our right. It didn't hit us, but it could have.

The fighters that we were refueling were, as I recall, doing targets in North Vietnam. There were fighters bombing in northern South Vietnam but were not assigned to our refueling mission. A fighter wing was stationed at Danang Air Base on the coast, and they did the in-country bombing and strategic bombing in that area.

After six weeks or so, we would rotate back to Lockbourne and come back through Guam. One of our happier duties was bringing back a hundred or more soldiers who had left their tour and were heading home. We would pile them into the back of the plane and take them to Hickam Field. They were the happiest guys you have ever seen. Most of them had a big Sony tape recorder and all their other junk. We looked like a Walmart. We were happy to have them, and they didn't care where we put them. They were sitting in uncomfortable side seats with straps but didn't care. They were headed home! From Hickam, we would fly straight back to Lockbourne. We did not escort any planes back on these trips.

We didn't actually have alert status in Thailand. Our missions were scheduled. When we got back from a typical mission, and before going back to the trailer to shower, we went by operations and were told what our schedule would be for the next day. Since we already knew what our mission would be, all we needed to know was what time the next day, morning or afternoon or both.

I would say that in a thirty-day month, we probably flew an average of thirty-five missions. All of them were during the day except for a couple of night missions, which was when the B-52s were doing the carpet bombing. I spent about a year in Thailand in intervals of six weeks each.

I moved over to what was called the "left seat", or pilot, my last eight months. Our wing was winding down, and so I did not go back to Thailand as an aircraft commander. I flew to the Philippines and to Goose Bay, among other places, as a commander, though.

I got out in November of 1968. Then I went to Cumberland Law School and finished in two-and-a-half years. While there, I flew for the Alabama Air National Guard, flying RF-84s, which were old Korea-war vintage single-seat planes designed to fly reconnaissance missions. Consequently, my first flight in the RF-84 was solo, which would have been intimidating but for my previous flying experience. Oddly enough, during this period I was frequently refueled by KC-135s, which were in a wing stationed at the Nashville airport. There was one difference. The RF-84 did not refuel like an F-4 Phantom. It had a probe of its own sticking out of the wing which meant the tanker would drop down a boom. At the end of the boom was a basket about three feet across. I would have to fly the end of the probe into the end of the basket. It was hard for a while because you were using your peripheral vision to hit the basket, stabbing and stabbing at it. The last couple of years we had to do it at night. The only references were the little light on the top of the basket and a little light on the end of the probe. It was kind of like trying to fly your probe into a laundry basket in the night. I would come off those missions just drenched with sweat.

After I graduated from law school, I was studying for the bar exams. I was up to my ears in studying for that. They retired our RF-84s and brought in a retired wing of RF-4 Phantoms, a huge monster of a supersonic plane. They had patches in the fuselage and wings from where they had been shot in Vietnam. I had a chance to fly them, but the training period was too long, and I just didn't have time. So I was in the service about eight-and-a-half years when I let the National Guard go.

I moved to Scottsboro in July of 1971 to practice law. I was a trial lawyer for twenty-three years, then was appointed circuit judge in April of 1994. I was elected unopposed in June of that year and remained a judge until 2006, when I retired.

I feel like my military service was one of the highlights of my life. I was fortunate enough to get through it without injury. I had several friends who didn't make it. I had two classmates in pilot training who were shot down over North Vietnam. My service made me so appreciative of our way of life and am just happy I could serve as long as I did. I thought about making it a career for a long time, but the SAC was not conducive to family life. We were gone so much, and when we weren't, we were pulling alert duty. Out of any given month, I probably had ten days at home.

How do I feel about the Vietnam war in retrospect? I admire the courage of those men over there. I think, however, having lost 58,000 young men, it was not worth the cost. It was a political war. I think we probably could have won it in the sense that we would have a permanent truce if the politicians had allowed the military to do its job. I'm not talking nuclear war but continuing the pressure on North Vietnam with the bombing. But in hindsight, I think it probably was not worth the cost.

Ron Gardner

An article in the Anniston Star explains that Engineman Third Class Ronald W. Gardner was the cannon-gunner aboard a heavily armed and armored gunboat similar to the famed ironclads of the Civil War. The gunboat was part of the unique Army/Navy Mobile Riverine Force that prowled the Mekong Delta, seeking out Viet Cong main force units and denying them use of the myriad network of waterways. Members of the Riverine Force were known as "river-rats" and, as evident in Ron's account, were involved in many firefights. Also evident is his extensive reflection on the war: the Vietnamese, the frustration at the limitations placed on the military, and the problems faced by returning Vietnam War veterans. He received multiple medals for the firefights in which he participated.

I am Ronald Winston Gardner. I was born in Jacksonville, Alabama, on February 3, 1947. I was raised and went to school outside of Jacksonville. The last three years of school I drove a school bus. Like everybody else, I was drafted after high school, but joined the Navy instead. I was nineteen.

I went to San Diego for my basic, then went to the USS Ogden, which was based in San Diego. It was an LTD, which landed personnel. The back lowered down. I then went to Vietnam by ship. I wound up off the coast of South Vietnam for fifty-nine days. We sent in fresh marines and also equipment.

I volunteered for a special school when they came around asking people to sign up. We didn't know where we would be going or anything like that. I ended up at Mair Island, out of San Francisco, which is a marine training center. I wound up going through boot camp again, since I was in this special program. We basically went through everything that Special Forces go through, such as gunnery training, setting booby traps, and survival. We were flown to the California desert for the gunnery training for three weeks. From there we went to Whidbey Island, Washington, where they dropped us off and left us for fourteen days for survival training.

Anybody who goes through Special Forces survival like at Whidbey knows it is the last thing you do in this training. They drop you in there, and you are on your own. You can quit anytime. We had a fish hook, a string, twenty feet of rope, shoes, five matches, a knife, and a roll of wire. I lived and survived, but I lost a lot of weight. We slept in parachutes, and we used the rope to keep it off the ground. The wire was for making snares so we could catch wild animals, and we did. Once we built a fire, we kept it going, and they taught us how to cook stuff and not stay around while it was being cooked. We were also taught a lot of evasion stuff. Then for the third week, they captured us and put us in a prison camp. What they did to us was unbelievable, but we knew we had to do it. You believed you were in a communist camp. They had you convinced of that. Even though we were in the Navy, they gave us this kind of training because they sent us straight to Vietnam.

We flew to Saigon on Braniff Air Lines, then flew down to Vinh Long. From there we went to Dong Tam, a base that may not be there any more. This was either late 1967 or early 1968. We actually took the boats off the merchant marine ships out there in the gulf, cranked them up, and drove them to Vinh Long, got out, and mounted our guns. We had to put on ammunition and storage items. The boats had nothing on them when we got them.

We were then dispersed in different groups in the delta. There were seven guys on my boat. It was a sixty-five-foot gunboat, which was like none you've ever seen. It had twin 50s on the front and twin 671s inside. I was a gunner and the engine man but everybody had to do everything, like being a medic and driving the boat. We were all assigned a gun, and one guy was in charge of the ammunition and had to make sure it was at the right gun. When you have seven guys on a boat, they all have to know what everybody else does because you never know if one of them is going to be disabled or something. There was not an officer on the boat. We had a chief, who was the boat captain, and he had the responsibility of taking the boat out and getting it in.

Something kind of funny happened a few days after we got on the boat. Davis was from Texas and had one of these big moustaches that turned way out. He waxed it all the time. We had been working around the clock getting our boat ready and were just exhausted. Davis laid down and went to sleep on the deck. One guy got scissors from the surgical bag and went up there and cut his moustache. Then somebody tickled his nose and woke him up. We all jumped to the side because he wanted to kill us all. We were always doing stunts like that.

We did not lose any from our crew, but several were lost in the squadron. I took a couple of the bodies to Ton Son Nhut Airbase in the back of a pickup truck. We come to this massive hangar that cannot be described. It may have been as big as five or six football fields. On one side were marble tables, one end to the other, and they were staggered. On the other side, as high as you could go, were caskets. Down in the end were boxes with flags on them. They were to the ceiling. When we brought these two guys in, they made us stay there until the two were tagged. The dog tags were put on their toes. The papers from the billfolds were taken out, and they gave us the information to take back to the commander. It was a shocking thing to know that you might be one of them on that table. I never forgot that. It was shocking to me.

In Vietnam, it sounds like it would be a good thing to be on the water, but you imagine that in the monsoons it is raining so hard the barrel of a gun would dump water in your lap almost enough to drown you. I've seen it raining so hard you couldn't see the boat right in front of you. Fifteen minutes later the sun would be shining. This would last for three months.

When I was on the boat, my main gun was a double-ought buckshot, and when you are close enough to somebody to shoot them with double-ought buckshot, you're pretty close to them. So you know you look them in the eye when you shoot. I never shot from my shoulders, always from the hip. I carried an M-16 that was assigned to me. When you got into a firefight, it ended so quick that it was almost over before it started.

The boat had no cover, and we slept down in the hold, which was protected from the elements. Other than that, there wasn't any protection. If you were on a gun mount or anything, you weren't covered, and anytime we were moving, we were close by that gun, monsoon or not.

We were a Navy outfit but were hated by every group. Although in the Navy, we were attached to the 52nd Brigade of the 9th Infantry. It was joint Army/Navy and was a new thing. We were supposed to be breaking up supply routes in the rivers and tributaries. In the delta area in South Vietnam, the roads were so swampy they were not very good, so most of the travel was by boat. The VC was moving up and down rivers in sampans and things like that. So our job was to break up these supply routes and communications and also insert military in these areas so they could go inland. We were also used as decoys, too. They put us out in the water like a duck to help determine where the enemy was, and if we got shot at, we would call the helicopter squadron to come in and get us out. We were not actually Swift boats. They were along the coast and didn't ordinarily run the rivers. We were inside in the small rivers and little tributaries.

We didn't just stay in the Mekong Delta area. We went all the way up to Saigon and even as far north as you could go on rivers. Let me tell you something about the rivers. They were tricky because they went up and down with the tide, so you had to know how much the water was up when you went in. If you went in during low tide, you wouldn't get out. Any time we had boats go in an area and get in a firefight, the boats would sit high and dry if the tide went down, leaving the boat like a sitting duck to the VC. This happened many times, and somebody had to go in and get them out. This happened to me two or three times. Once we had gone in and had a special tugboat boat with us, because we knew the tide was going out, and it would be close. We tied three boats together and then had the tugboat hook on to us. It dragged us through the marshes into the water. But while it was pulling us, our engines were doing what they could, but we were sucking mud. We were changing filters down inside, trying to get them cleared up so we wouldn't burn out our engines. We knew if we didn't get out, we were stuck until the tide come back, and this was not a comfortable feeling.

We would normally take three or four boats and go to a certain area. We might be gone for a couple of weeks, or even three or four weeks. Sometimes we were gone as long as six weeks. We lived on the boat all this time. We'd go up these rivers, and when we'd come into contact with the VC, our first job was to pin them down if we could. We had the firepower. We had a flame thrower that shot napalm a hundred yards away and fifteen yards wide, and it could shoot for six minutes. That was in one of our boats. We had one that had a 105 rifle, which was a cannon that could pretty well do some damage. We had the twin 50s on the front of our boat as well as a Mark 19 grenade launcher. Then we had two aircraft 20s mounted on each side, so we could pretty well defend ourselves for a little bit. After our missions were over, all the boats would go in, and we'd go to briefings and things like that, just getting ready for the next operation. We could also take a shower and refresh ourselves and buy personal items.

Yes, we did get sick, all of us did, with the flu or something. I didn't get injured or get any purple hearts, even though my boat was blown up several times.

We actually went off the boat and did reconnaissance from our boat. We went in to get people out and bring them back, not only our service people, but civilians as well. Once we got into a firefight and a little girl was seriously injured. It was a joint operation with us and the South Vietnamese. We went and got her out. She was blown up pretty bad. She had been in a rice paddy with a water buffalo and got caught in the middle of the firefight. We put her on our boat to get her evacuated and out of there. The general of the South Vietnamese Army said no, they would put her in a sampan and get her out their way. He said she should not have been out there first of all and that he couldn't jeopardize his operation for one little girl. Our commander and all of us were crying because she was tore up pretty bad. Actually, our commander begged him to let us take her, but he still said no.

We saw a lot of things like that and saw what the Viet Cong could do. If you see it firsthand over there, you can see that it could even happen in our country. Those people have no thought of life and no thought of who they killed or why they killed. They only know they are ordered to kill. Once I saw they had hit an orphanage, and we leveled their boat when they came back because they said if they saw an American flag again over that orphanage, they would come back and finish what they had started. So we waylaid them.

But we were limited in what we could do. If you saw the map I saw, it had green, red, yellow, and blue. Areas were marked so we would know which areas in which we could fire, not fire, or that our mission was to fire. In some areas, you weren't allowed to fire at all if it was close to a town or in a village. These no-fire zones in the rivers we were on meant we couldn't fire in any circumstances, even if you were being fired on. We had to call and try to get out of there if we could. The VC had our maps so they knew where they could shoot at us and would catch us there.

I think the reason for these limits was that it was not a war, it was a police action. Once over there, we were missing for forty-five days on a secret operation that I am not allowed to talk about, and I don't know much of it myself. All I do know is that we were taking people into places we weren't supposed to be, and nobody even knew where we were. We did this several times during that period. But anyway, we couldn't get or send any mail or contact anybody. My mother went to Congressman Nichols and told him her son was over there fighting in the war in Vietnam. He told her it was not a war but a police action. She said I was not a policeman, so you bring him home. She was mad. After we got back from being missing, congressmen were on the backs of everyone.

One time we were on a mission when our boat was blown up and towed back to the camp. It was lifted out of the water and being worked on. We were staying in a building with a MARS, or Mobile Amateur Radio Service, where you could call home. I was in that office at eleven-thirty at night fixing to make a phone call home, when an air raid whistle went off. The enemy knew where we were, and the whole squadron had to come back because four boats had been damaged. They blew up the town we were in. I got out of the building, and when I looked back it wasn't there any more. It had been incinerated. It was near a fuel dump that had exploded.

I'll tell you how firefights were. On our missions, it was kind of like riding down the road and somebody taking a pot shot at you. You don't know where it came from or what happened. All you know is that you won't be able to duck. So we concentrated all our power toward that area from where you received fire. One time when we were moving a squadron up the river, they made us go to a town we called the "Brick Factory". Anyway, we were coming up and we were turning to go up one of these little tributaries. As we went through, they hit the front and back boats and decommissioned them. They really let loose on us. They were shooting at us while standing in town where people were shopping and everything, and it looked like there wasn't anything going on. They were shooting B-50 rockets, RPG rounds, machine guns, and AK-47s from the bank. We finally decided we were gonna die right there, and if we hadn't returned fire, we would have. It was a no-fire zone. Our commander was on board at that time, and he told us take them out because we had to get out of there. So when we opened fire, the enemy was shocked when they saw that we were shooting back and taking them out. That is how firefights were. The most likely places to get hit were the places you weren't supposed to get hit. The enemy was waiting on you, because he knew you would be reluctant to shoot at him. You were allowed to at least defend yourself, though.

Were the civilians helping them? Let me put it this way. We were outsiders, but the VC spoke their language. That is like having Yankees come down here to the south. You probably can't pick out the southern accent from the northern accent unless you are from the United States, and you couldn't pick out the VC from a group of people unless you were Vietnamese and understood their customs and slang. I don't think the civilians were supporting them, but they knew that if they turned against them, they would be shot. So they couldn't afford to trust us because we were going to leave them, even though we helped them and defended them. If they did, they knew the VC would come back in and slaughter them. We went into several villages where people, including kids, were cut up and mutilated. You can't imagine. It's hard for me to talk about it, because you wouldn't believe it. But here's the thing. If they would do that do their own, what would they do to us? That is what scared you so much. You felt so bad for the people, though, because they were trapped. They were damned if they did and damned if they didn't. This is kind of the way we were when drafted into service. There was no other choice.

The VC were dressed like everybody. They blended in and you couldn't pick them out, and the civilians wouldn't point them out. Then we would capture the civilians, and they would say they were going to be on our side. So we took them as scouts. I know those scouts shot at us at night. They would pat you on the back in the day time and still shoot you when it got dark. We were worse than gullible. We were stupid because we believed it when these people said they were going to be our friends, but they weren't. That was to save their own hide.

What I am about to say is my true feelings, and I was told this by a Vietnamese general riding on our boat. He said if the United States had never come in, the Vietnamese could have won that war. But with the US pulling back on them like a team of horses, it was like the Vietnamese wanted to be running wide open but were being held back to where they couldn't get into a full gallop. Every time they did, they were thought to be unmerciful. There is no mercy in war.

We worked with the ARVN, or South Vietnamese Army. We worked on joint operations, and we carried them in and dropped them off. We had interpreters on our boat. Our way of getting information was going and asking. Theirs was to take possible sources of information up in a helicopter. If the first one doesn't talk, throw him out. The second would then talk. But we didn't do that. The ARVN said they could get information, and methods like that were how. We couldn't do it that way. We were trying to be too good, and you can't be a good guy in war.

Because of things like this, when I came back, I didn't believe I was alive. Sometimes, even today, it is hard for me to believe I lived through what I did and came back. It was not a pretty sight. You would be going down the river minding your own business and having a good time, when all of a sudden the whole world around you exploded. It might even happen as we cruised down the river at night, and suddenly the sky would light up. Many times I heard "Puff the Magic Dragon" call over the radio, asking if we needed any ammunition, and we would say to fire it. Then it would look like a stairway all the way to the ground when he was shooting. The tracers coming out of the side of that plane were a pretty sight in a firefight. You were always glad to see them because usually we were out there without any support around. When the helicopters came, they had a distinctive sound. When you are in the middle of something, that is the sweetest sound you will ever hear.

Some nights we would go to the ship I'll tell you about in a minute.

We had four boats that would take off and go around this ship all night long. Our boats took turns doing this, kind of like being on watch. What we did was every fifteen minutes we would launch a concussion grenade in the water. The bomb would explode, and we hoped it would kill any VC swimmers coming out to bomb the ship. We did have ships blown up like that. We had a firefight one time while we were doing this.

When I was over there, we listened to a radio station that came on every morning. It was called "Good morning, Vietnam". In the movie, they didn't say what was said on the station, which was, "Good morning, Vietnam. Today we expect to lose 362 men. Don't you be one of them". That is really what they said. They actually estimated how many were going to die that day. Robin Williams never said that, but I heard it lots of times. A TV station there had a girl who came and did the welcome. Her name was Candy and she always wore a different bathing suit. If we could ever get close to a TV, we wanted to watch that. She was really my only connection to stateside. She was always sweet and did a wonderful job, and I wish someone could find her and tell her there is one person who remembers her.

As far as my feelings are concerned, while I was in Vietnam, the hotel we were in the night we landed in Saigon was bombed, and it scared me. This was during the Tet Offensive. Right after we picked up our boats, we had two or three firefights, and I had a feeling then that I wasn't coming home. I knew then, and I just didn't give a crap. You just get to where you don't care. You know your time is coming. You just don't worry about it. You try to keep your head down and do what's right. But, boy, I'm nineteen years old and you give me a gun and a speedboat, and I'll show you what I can do. You know what I'm saying? In a way, we were just having fun. We went out and we played and skied and did whatever we wanted to. You know, we were daring them a lot of times, because we really didn't care until the last two weeks. These are the most terrifying times of your life because you start thinking, "I have almost made it, but am I really going to get out?" They didn't take us out that early. We were in the field until three days before we came home. Our boat was released, and I never saw the guys on my boat again.

I wasn't even sure I had ever been in Vietnam, because I had no good way to confirm it. But then I signed up for the Mobile Riverine paper when I was reading the Stars and Stripes one time. Well, it wasn't two weeks until I got a call. It was one of the guys, and I called him an "egg sucking dog" because he loved sucking eggs. We'd steal anything we could get from the galley ship, including eggs. The ship was out in the river, and we tied on to it but weren't allowed to go on it. But we'd sneak up there and steal stuff; then we'd get on our boat and cook it. We could make a stove by taking toilet paper and diesel fuel and putting it in a gallon jug. Light it and you got a good stove. We would try to cook a meal, because no cooking facilities were on our boat.

The food we had when we were out was C-rations, K-rations, and dehydrated food. We would take a canteen and put it on the manifold of the engine down in the hole of the boat. We left it all day to get the water hot, then poured it in the dehydrated food, closed it up for about five minutes, and you had a warm meal of beef and rice or chicken and rice or spaghetti. The worst was when the beans didn't get soft and you'd almost break a tooth on them. We got supplies from this big ship called the "Big Apple" that was moved by tugboats on the river. On the side were barges, eight or nine on each time. Our boats would pull up to the barges and tie off and then load down with C-rations and whatever we could get. We'd also get a fresh supply of fuel and water and ammo. Then we went back out.

I was over there a year and was on that boat almost all the time. I did go to Cam Ranh Bay on R&R for about five days. I was supposed to get off again for R&R, but that was during the Tet Offensive, and nobody was getting out of there.

We had radios on board, and we would call in "Arabian night 1","Arabian night 2", or "Debra's Foxtrot", which was the code for "Puff the Magic Dragon". We would call and try to get one of them. If they picked us up, they would say, "We'll bring what we got", and then come over us. The copter pilots sat nearly on top of us. When over us, they would head toward the area the fire was coming from and sweep it with mini-guns, which sound like somebody cranking up a model airplane. Their rockets would land in those areas. If we secured an area, we would move on, and troops would be dropped there to see what damage had been done and clean up the mess.

Every group worked together. Sometimes, the helicopter pilots would get shot down, and we went in after them in the jungle. Sometimes, we took the pilots by boat to a destination. Once we spent six weeks at a Green Beret outpost. I remember we picked up nine of the pilots and took them to where we were going. We thought that was great until we did get to where we were headed. Three of them refused to get off because we got into a massive firefight. The others did get off and were able to go in and do their job, but those who wouldn't get off came back with us. You don't know what it's like. One moment it's quiet and everything is going great, but then it changes. There is no place to hide on those boats. Nothing protects you from a rocket, even the armor on our boats. It will hit, explode, and burn its way through any armor. We had several men in our squadron killed that way.

One time a special was being done on us by some media because our company had just started in 1967 when the Mobile Riverine Force was formed and activated. So we were one of the first to go in there. Since it was new, we didn't really know what our job was except to do whatever we had to do to get back out. That was Job One.

Agent Orange was sprayed in that area. We saw those big planes come in and spray over us and along the banks. Yeah, we were sprayed several times. I did develop leukemia, and I have other problems, too. They are working on deciding if they might be related to Agent Orange.

When I got home, I began to realize that people don't understand the cost of freedom as we know it. I gave a talk one time and this is what I said: "I remember most of all the fact that the flag we see was laid across 57,000 coffins, and when you see that flag you remember that those men died for your freedom. You say they just died, but along with them died their heritage, their future generations, everything. They gave the ultimate price. I have kids. I have grandkids. They gave up everything for our freedom."

Coming back from Vietnam was a lot different from coming back from WWII. In WWII, the veterans came back together, whole companies or whole ships. So they could talk among themselves and discuss things and realize it was real. In Vietnam, you had a billet number, and when your time was up, you came back, not with the same people you went over there with or served with. That is why I questioned myself for a long time whether I had even been there or not. I was the only person who knew, and I couldn't confirm it except for the Anniston Star newspaper clippings my mother had saved. This was my only reality. A lot of guys came back and didn't know for sure, either, and needed closure that they had been in a combat zone. A lot of them committed suicide. We had a man that lived down here by the side of the river. He was a disabled veteran and would not even come to town. He died on that river. Nobody could fool with him or mess with him. He could not come back to society.

Let me say something about the guys who were over there. I believe the "ground pounders", or "jarheads", which were marines, had it rough, bad rough. We had it bad, but we didn't have to get off that boat much, have jungle rot to deal with, and all that stuff. We were on a flat surface. When we got off into the jungle, we could get back on that boat. We had dry clothes sometime, but they had to live with what they had on. When they came on board, they stunk, but I never thought of them as stinking. I was proud of that stink because I knew they were probably safe, and I could take them back to clean up. You can get rid of stink, but you can't get rid of death. Those guys did the big jobs. All we did was get them to where they could do their big jobs. I'm proud of every man who served over there, whatever they did. They are all very important.

When we left Vietnam, I came back to the US on leave. I was guaranteed shore duty anywhere in the country. But the day my leave was up, my orders came, and I was told I couldn't stay in the states, so I had to leave. They sent me to the Philippines, and I stayed there the remaining eight months of my tour as a backup for those in Vietnam. I was called one day and told I was going to a dress-white inspection. The reason was that they got me out there in front of everybody, and they had medals that were coming from Vietnam and had finally caught up with me. There were nine citations, eleven commendations, and meritorious unit citations from our commander for operations we did in certain areas. We were in fifteen campaigns, and they read every one of them. On the Vietnam Service Medal are stars. Only three would fit on mine, but eleven actually came. These were the number of firefights I was in that they knew about, but all the skirmishes I was involved in were not included. So we were in a lot of operations.

When I got out, I came to work for my dad, who had a plumbing company. We were mechanical contractors. Then I went on to college and graduated from Baptist Theological College in Florida. I was a minister for a while, but got out of that and built my own plumbing company here in Scottsboro. I was able to raise three Christian boys.

When I came back from overseas, there were months that my mother and my dad didn't know if I was going to live or not. You go into a war zone, you come back, and people act like you are nobody, a baby killer, someone who shot innocent people, or you were this or that. You are tagged with that. Most of the time I was shooting was not to kill somebody, but to help us get away from whatever was after us so we wouldn't be killed ourselves. So when we came back, it was a shock to find out that what we thought were good deeds was what we were hated for. People don't understand this, but Jane Fonda and others like her hurt our military more than you will ever know.

This is why I say that. I was in the Tet Offensive. They blew my boat out of the water. I ended up in a Green Beret outpost. We had nothing but the clothes on our back. We sat there for three days, shooting mortars, trying to keep the enemy from overrunning the camp. They were coming at us with everything they had. We found out that Congress had shut down all backup to military personnel because of Jane Fonda and the others. I lost several buddies that day just in that short time, and she was the one who was able to maneuver the military away from us. No B-52s, no fly-ins, not nothing. They were backing Jane Fonda, not us. We were just left hanging. Do you know how it feels to be in a foreign country and know that your country has turned its back on you? So we came back feeling hurt, but finally we put things back together and got things moving. We don't need to get into that situation again, and that is why I am reluctant to stick troops in if they are not going all the way. Let's not play this Vietnam game again. We haven't learned the lesson. We did the same thing in Iraq. We put our men in harm's way and set them out there as sitting targets, the same as in Vietnam.

I couldn't go for a job interview. When they heard you had been to Vietnam, they didn't want you. It was hard for a veteran to get hired, even though we had served this country. Here is the thing about it. We did not ask to go. We were ordered by our government to go over there and serve our country under a draft. We would be prosecuted if we didn't go.

I have no idea if the war was worth it. I don't know how we accomplished anything there, I really don't. I feel like this. We paid a high price for nothing. You have to understand, we had to stop at the DMZ. If they would have let us go on into North Vietnam, we would have won.

Richard Carlile

Richard Carlile was an advisor to South Vietnamese units ranging in size from platoons to battalions, and he went with them on multiple missions. In his 270 days as an advisor, he estimated his unit was involved in a firefight on all but two of them. On his last mission, he was hit a total of six times over a nine hour period. He received multiple medals, including three Bronze Star Medals with "V" Device.

I am Richard Carlile. I was born on Jan 18, 1945, in Birmingham, Alabama. I graduated from Ramsay High School and the University of Alabama in Tuscaloosa. Then I went into the military.

I had been in ROTC and went into the military as a second lieutenant in 1967. I had to go to Fort Benning for basic infantry officer training. From there, I went to Fort McClellan, Alabama, and worked in the G-3 section, which is operations. I was a training inspector, checking classes that were given to make sure they were pertinent and that time wasn't being wasted and that sort of thing.

From there, I was selected to go to flight school in Fort Walters, Texas, out in the middle of nowhere. We flew choppers and stuff like that. I have to say I liked that. My friends and I who went on flights of our own would do some things like flying underneath overpasses, just to see if we could do it. We found out those choppers could do a lot of things like that. I was coming in for a landing one day, and all of a sudden an instructor pilot came out after I landed and asked what I was doing. I asked what he meant, and he said I came in at the wrong angle. I said I didn't think so, and we went back up and flew in again. I scared the living daylights out of him. He said we were very close to doing something called settling with power, which means falling out of the air. My angle of approach had been too sharp. So I was checked for my eyesight and discovered that I had a problem with depth perception. After that, I was told I couldn't fly, that it was too dangerous.

I got my choice to go to any other special school, so I went to Fort Bragg and knew I would be going to Vietnam with the Military Assistance Command Vietnam, or MACV. For this, I needed to speak Vietnamese, so I went to language school. Then, I was off to Vietnam. We were getting ready to land in Saigon when all of sudden the plane took off again. This was during the Tet Offensive, and the airport was under attack. In due course, we landed and were taken to a large compound. We were in a foreign country and didn't know the situation and thought we should be getting weapons now. But we did not get weapons now. It was night, and some of the guys had been there before and were telling war stories. I was listening, and some of them were pretty interesting. Then all of a sudden these explosions started going off. I'm thinking "My gosh! I'm here, those suckers are going to end up coming in here and I don't have a weapon except a knife I had from my father-in-law." So, okay, I'm going to be prepared to use it. I looked out the door and saw two guys heading down a ditch-thing, running and wearing black uniforms. Those people were Viet Cong and were apparently killed a little later after being caught in a storm drain.

Finally, they took us to get what we needed, like uniforms, weapons, and that sort of thing. This made me feel pretty good until I realized we had no ammo. Shortly, we got on a plane and they flew us to Can Tho, IV Corps headquarters. We were not issued ammo when we first flew into there. While at Can Tho, we slept in bunks with nets around them. I wondered what they were for. It seemed like they would restrict the air or something. Yep, I did decide I wanted them.

That first night, the VC hit us. I thought I was going to get some sleep until then. I grabbed my weapon out, and there was a hole in the wall. I didn't have any ammo. I asked where was the ammo and was told we didn't get any if there was no enemy around because they didn't want people getting shot inside here by their comrades. I thought he was kidding, but that was the way it worked. Finally the firing was over.

The next day we got clearance, if you will, to fly into Vi Thanh Province on one of the funniest aircrafts I've ever seen. It could take off in the shortest distance and land in the shortest distance. It could get in the air faster than anything I've ever seen. The people flying it were unique, too, and I got to be friends with several of them over a period of time. I processed in and was told I was going to Du Long District.

I learned that the organization of the units in the area was something like this. You had a province team composed of all sorts of stuff like communications; shotguns (which were people attached to it who flew little fixed-wing aircraft which directed artillery in); Air Force types attached from time to time doing air strikes, which were more effective because their communications were directly with the jets; attached helicopter support; and things like that.

Then you had district teams. There were five or six of these. I was on a district team. We had a district senior advisor; an assistant senior advisor, which was me; an operations NCO; a radio/telephone operator; a security officer; and a medic. That was it. Underneath the district team you had people who lived with, trained, and advised the assigned unit, called MAT Teams, which were Mobile Advisory Teams. We only had one of these, and they got shot up a lot

I was being driven from Vi Thanh down the road to Duc Long and saw all those people in black. I asked if all of them were enemy and was told they weren't because that was the cheapest material; therefore it was the peasant dress. In our training, we had been accustomed to thinking everyone in black was the enemy. The truth was, you couldn't tell who was who.

Finally, I got to the Duc Long district headquarters, which was a building with a stove in it of sorts so you could actually heat something up. There were beer and coke and water, but no ice. There was an ancient refrigerator that operated off of gas. We had about an eight-man barrack with cots, but that was all we really needed. There was an area with a radio that was where things in the district were run. So, that was it.

I was told I couldn't go out into the field on missions until I was acclimated. My assistant was the operations NCO and security

NCO. We were being oriented and told what our team and individual responsibilities were. But I still had to wait ten days or so before I could do anything like go out on an operation. Well, on day two, a weird thing happened. A guy in another unit got sick on site and couldn't go, which meant the whole operation was going to be cancelled because you had to have an American with the Vietnamese units. So I told them I would be there in twenty minutes, you won't have to cancel it. I head up there and go on that operation. I did not realize those operations were like twelve hours or better, and some I have been on were as much as forty-eight hours. The operations were seek and destroy, not search and clear. If we found VC in a village and they wouldn't surrender, we basically would search and destroy. That was the whole idea. I was an advisor to South Vietnamese troops.

So I go out on my first mission. We were walking through swamps, rice paddies, and hard ground, which was rough on your feet. Like on other missions, you didn't try to dry your feet because you were walking in water so much they wouldn't stay dry anyway. We received some enemy fire that day. It was a sniper from twelve o'clock, and we ran into an enemy unit of ten to twelve about a click later, so we knew they were in the area. I was standing on top of this rice paddy, and Sergeant McGinnis, who was my operations NCO, was just in front of me. I heard this sound, like a crack and a whoosh. I asked what that was. About then McGinnis hits me in the lowest part of my legs, and I go down behind the dike into the paddy. He told me what I had heard was a bullet going past my ear. So that is how I found out what a bullet going past you sounds like. He told me that I now qualified for a Combat Infantry Badge, and it was only my first mission. We did have a small firefight. The Vietnamese I was with and advising were not doing exactly what they should have been doing, so I showed them what they should be doing. In so doing, they learned a little, but I learned something too. I learned that I should be showing their leaders what to do, and it worked. Their company commander and I turned out being really good friends. We raised his kill ratio from about five to one to sixty to one, which is enemy killed versus his Vietnamese troops killed.

Anyway, we got back from the operation, and I didn't realize how tired I was because of the adrenalin flowing. I went to sleep and woke up about thirty hours later. My boss wasn't happy that I had gone out before the ten days were up. I was not acclimated to the heat. I know that one day, because of this heat, I lost ten pounds. Going through what we went through that first day, I decided, was not like just going for a walk. I understood better about all of this, and I learned that my troops needed rest after going out. From then on, we would go to certain points, then stop. This worked better than not stopping because the troops were rested and could do things more efficiently.

My thoughts about my first day out were still that I thought it was going to be easy, because when we drove in we saw these people with black pajamas who appeared to be friendly. I figured that when we went out, we would know when to hit them, which was not the case as it turned out.

We had 270 operational days. Only on two days we did not find anything. Other than that, we found something like the VC or NVA. In other words, we had contact with the enemy, and by contacts, I'm talking about firefights. One reason for all these contacts is that we broke our units down and went on multiple paths. If somebody ran into trouble, we had other people we could send who could eliminate the problem very quickly.

The Vietnamese with us might be only ten or so, which was an intel unit, to maybe 300. Earlier I mentioned the Americans in the unit, but we never had more than two on missions. So it would be me plus either the operations officer or the radio man. Sometimes, the security officer might be there, but he never went with the same company all the time.

We would never do the same thing twice. We might set up a squad on an ambush, sometimes even multiple ambushes. But the VC would often find out where the ambushes were and avoid them. I finally realized what we needed to do. We would set up an ambush before nightfall. We wanted whoever was alerting the VC about our location to see us, hoping they would tell the VC where we were. After nightfall, we would move the ambush. This tactic proved valuable. We were also able to pick up documents that would tell what the enemy was doing. We would try to find the enemy, isolate them, and then try to get them to give up. If they didn't give up, we would do whatever was necessary.

We had one operation in which we went into Cambodia because the enemy had a radio tower there that was used to provide information to the North Vietnamese about the goings on in the area. Our mission was to take this radio station down. We went in with a ten-man unit. We knew the radio tower was there, and we knew it was functioning, but they had moved, and we couldn't find it at first. When we did locate the team with the radio, we simply destroyed everything so they couldn't give out the needed information that the enemy used to infiltrate into South Vietnam. That was one type operation.

There were other type missions. One time we found an NVA training battalion. That was one of the weirdest missions I went on. As we were heading to this location, we talked about how strange that area was. We did not know what it was, but you could tell it was dangerous and big. All the things that should be normal weren't in place, like no birds were singing and insects were not moving. The company commander said today might be our last. I asked him what he was talking about. He said he didn't know if we would get out of this one. I told him I was. Then he told me all air support had been cut off. It was being redirected somewhere else. I said that I wasn't aware of that, so I radioed and was told there was action going on in a certain place, and the air support was being diverted. I told them I wanted that air support because it was needed back here. I was told they couldn't come. So I told them I was returning to Du Lac now. They said I couldn't do that. I told his air support supervisor the same. Finally, they said they could give us one round of air support.

So we went out there, and Good Lord, we had nine of our South Vietnamese guys get knocked down, or maybe it was ten, at one time. When I realized what was happening, I told our guys to stop and get down, because all of them had been shot in the stomach. They were screaming, wanting to be pulled out. This made me think somebody knew what they were doing, all having been hit in the gut. We were in trouble if they could just pick us off like flies. So I got on the phone and said I wanted the air support now, but all they could come up with was a heavy fire team. The Cobras did come in and were receiving fire. Finally, we did get the kind of support we needed. I told the helicopter commander I needed to pick up some kind of rhythm with them as they were going in, and I thought I could get our wounded out if we established this rhythm. So they came in a couple of times, and we could tell exactly when they were coming in and pulling out. So when the choppers came in firing, I took off. When the chopper pulled off, I dove and grabbed one of the injured South Vietnamese and started back when the copter came back in again. I kept repeating this process. As the battle went on, the enemy had a machine gun that was doing a number on us on the opposite side, so we went and took him out. The rest of it was fairly simple because B-52s and things like that were now available. They bombed the heck out of them, and we just basically sat back and watched. I received a Bronze Star Medal for this mission.

We did discover we had been tangling with a NVA battalion. They were kidnapping people and training them to be Viet Cong. They ripped them out of their homes. But we were able to stop that. We got all of their flags and other things. We found out that people would pay for the flags. For instance, members of the Air Force would pay a box of steaks for a couple of VC flags, or even a case of beer. So it got to the point where we made VC flags to use for trading items.

How did we know the enemy was around? Normally, there was something going on in the area, like animals were missing or things like that. We got to a point where we basically denied anybody the right to move at night. We used a Starlight, which was a device that could allow night vision. If something was spotted moving with the Starlight, you had to get authorization to fire. We would then take action, and when we checked it out, it would be what we thought it was.

One of the operations was called Snake River. A bunch of Americans had been destroyed at this river. It was one of the VC's favorite places, and they could operate fairly freely there. This operation was supposed to have been done by another unit, not mine. I happened to be in Vi Thanh that day, and they would soon be lifting off from the airport for the mission. I was asked if I could go since their advisor couldn't. It was going to be with a new regional forces company that had very little training. What we were going after was like ten VC, or that is what was suspected, anyway. We had fifty people, and there was another unit going with us. They also had fifty people, but they were going on the opposite side of a canal from us. We were to meet up at a particular point. The new company I was going with included the old executive officer of 113 Regional Forces Company that I already knew. I hadn't seen him in a while, but I liked the guy. He was kind of cool but weird sometimes. So I thought it might be interesting.

The reason I liked this guy was that he came up with some of the durndest things you ever heard of. If we were looking for the VC, he could literally tell us where we would find them. He'd be pointing at a map, and I was trying to figure out what he was seeing on the map. We actually ran into the VC at every point he said. It was amazing. He did this for about four or five operations, saving lives on our side. I asked his commander how he got that information. Finally, the commander told me the guy's son was giving him the information. So I was thinking something like this guy is sending his own son out to get it? You gotta be kidding, that's dangerous. So I asked the commander about that. He said the man's son had died ten years ago. Apparently, in his sleep, the son came and told him where to find the VC. I couldn't believe we had been trusting that.

Anyway, this guy was now with this new company I was going with, and I wanted to congratulate him on assuming the new command. But he didn't show up. I was told by his exec he was sick and wouldn't be going. I was thinking about his son and all, so I was concerned that we were going to run into something heavy. But we started our operation, and it was working perfectly. We ran into a couple of booby traps but were able to eliminate them without any problem. The canal that we and the other unit were along was a double horseshoe. The other unit gets hit on their side of the canal. I couldn't figure out then what was going on, but I did later. They were not staying in the tree line the way we were. They were heading right down the middle of that cotton-picking rice paddy to where they were supposed to go, but not the way they were supposed to go. That unit had an American second lieutenant and South Vietnamese troops.

Anyway, it looked like a lot of them were going to die, so I thought we needed to do something about this. Were there really only ten VC in a firefight with fifty of our men and inflicting such damage? I talked to my commander, and he still thought there were only ten of the enemy. So I decided this is what we are going to do. We will breach that canal and go across to the other side, and we'll take care of those ten real quick. So here we go. Guess what? It ended up being about five hundred instead of ten, and they were in concrete bunkers.

I get hit in the shoulder and couldn't use it any more after that. My interpreter got his brains blown out. Anyway, I'm barking out commands. I wanted the fire returned, so that is what we did. My radio operator went down, too, so I took the radio off of him and used it to call in artillery and air support. Then all of a sudden my radio got hit, knocking it out. I'm on this side of a dike in a rice paddy, in water. It ends up there was a sniper behind us. Apparently he was in a big jug in a corner of the rice paddy. The top was on with mud on the top of that. He would raise that top up and shoot, then put the cover back on so nobody could find him. Then he ended up hitting me right behind the ear. I go under water.

Finally, I come up out of the water. I look over at my partner, who was a sergeant I had just met, and he is bleeding in the face. He said he only got hit by a rock, but he thought I was dead, saying I had been under water for over a minute. So I told him I'm not dead and that we were getting out of this, and that he was to follow my lead and do exactly what I told him to do. Everything is timed, so you gotta do this thing just right. I told him to get on the other side of the dike and do it now. I don't know why, I just knew we had to get on the other side. So we did get on the other side, and we are crawling along the dike. We were heading towards a radio I had seen about a football field away from us. So here I am heading up that way, and suddenly there were some weird sounds, and alarms were going off in my head. I stopped, and all these rounds started hitting the water in front of us. Good Lord, over our heads, too, and stuff like that. I had a grenade launcher that I carried in addition to my M-16, but the M-16 was gone. I took that launcher and came over that dike. But the launcher was hit as I came up and was useless. It was lucky that it didn't blow up on me.

So I got back down. Then the alarms and weird noises stopped. So we take off to the next dike. Then the alarms go off again and here came another bunch of rounds. Finally, I got to where the radio was. So I put in the correct frequencies and called, saying I needed air support. So they answered OK and said they thought I was dead and all that kind of stuff, but it was going to take a while for the air support to get there. Suddenly, a heavy helicopter fire team Thunderbird pilot came on the radio and said he was en route and would be there shortly; just hang on. They came in and brought all kinds of things. They were superstars as far as I was concerned. They asked what was going on, and I said we are receiving fire when we shouldn't be receiving any at all, and that I thought they were in reinforced bunkers or something. Other helicopter fire teams came, too. The whole thing was gorgeous if you don't think about the viciousness of what was going on. Then they came with phosphorus and set that whole area on fire. They told me they might not be killing them, but were fixing it so they couldn't see. Oh yeah, I thought, you seem to be doing a pretty effective job.

I got hit a total of six times that day over a nine-hour period: my left arm; my shoulder, behind the ear (causing the loss of a piece of the ear); twice in the chest; and twice with shrapnel. I'm sitting in this little pool of water in the highest spot there so I could see what was going on. I was trying to stay low but would occasionally get up to try to see. When you do that, you take a chance. That is why I got hit so much. I realized the pool I was in was red, and then I realized it was my blood. A South Vietnamese medic was doing all he could to stop the bleeding. The guy probably saved my life. About nine o'clock at night, they brought Spooky up. Spooky is an aircraft that fires 50mm rounds, and, in about a minute, can cover every square foot of a football field. So any enemy movement out there was pretty well covered.

In the meantime, the Vietnamese 120th Regional Force and the Vietnamese 113th Regional Force, the two Vietnamese regional forces companies I had trained, came in and did a relief-in-force and got me out of there. A Medivac pilot came in. He was told he couldn't land because the area was too hot. He came in, anyway. We had helped him get out of some sticky situations in the past. He landed on a moonless night with no lights, including no lights for him. You can see how dangerous that could be. This guy came in during an active combat situation at night, no stars, no nothing. What we did was set a hooch on fire and gave him a reference to that hooch. It looked pretty to me. As we were getting out, the pilot got shot in the stomach. The pilot violated orders by being there. Court martial action was talked about, but he ended up getting a much-deserved Silver Star.

They brought me to Can Tho. I remember they were cutting my clothes off in a hurry, and I remember the rock-and-roll music that was being played in there. The people working on me were laughing, and I thought it was at my expense, and I didn't appreciate that. They used wire to stitch me up and put me back together as well as they could. I had been shot in the chest, missing my heart by the width of a fingernail, and another shot missed my lungs about as much. I also got the shrapnel because our air support was dropping 500 pound bombs within a hundred yards of where we were. I got shrapnel twice, and it is still working it's way out. I was lucky to get out alive.

The next day, I was still pretty hot about how they were joking around about me while sewing me up. A little nurse told me I had lost a lot of blood during the surgery the day before. I was also told that if you see some of the stuff they see in surgery, you have to do everything you can to keep a positive attitude, and it works. That changed my attitude then. I told the surgeons later that I appreciated them. They even presented me with all the bullets. Some guys came in a day or two later to award me the Purple Heart, the one award I didn't want.

After rehab, I was told I would have to go to Fort Sam Houston as a language instructor. The Vietnamese language I had learned before going to Vietnam helped me considerably. As I said earlier, I had an interpreter, but I could tell what the South Vietnamese said to him. I had one of the Vietnamese troops actually say he was going to shoot me when I turned my back. I turned around and immediately turned back around. That sucker was putting his weapon up. He didn't keep it up too long. That is all I need to say.

Another thing about my language training. My interpreter in the Snake River mission got shot, like I said. I was trying to talk to the Vietnamese troops but couldn't get them to understand. I thought I must be so excited that I was getting the Vietnamese language all garbled up or something. Later on, a guy was writing about this particular incident and asked me if there was anything I might want to know. I did want some information about that language problem. He said those soldiers were paid Cambodian soldiers and didn't speak Vietnamese.

I didn't want to go to Texas. I requested somewhere in Alabama and told them if I didn't get that, I was going to get out as soon as possible. I wound up at Fort McClellan as commander of the 3rd Army NCO Academy, which was a great assignment. All the people you were with were pros. From there, I went to Germany, then to Redstone Arsenal for about a year. I considered making the military a career, but I didn't like the politics. So I decided to get out. While at Redstone, I began formulating plans for the restaurant here in Scottsboro.

My thoughts about the Vietnamese War in retrospect are that we probably should have been there, but we should have finished what we started to do. I think that because we didn't finish it, we will be seeing the effects from now on. I don't want to see any soldiers go to combat at all, but if required, do it quickly and get out. We have not done a good job of avoiding that. What happened in Vietnam set the stage for the things that followed. We shouldn't have been in Iraq. Special Forces units could have taken care of that. We didn't need to send in all those troops. We have troops that are trained for such specific things, and we used to use them more.

I was lucky enough to walk out of Vietnam with three Bronze Stars. I also got a RCOM, which is an Army Commendation Medal, at the Arsenal. I also received the Vietnamese Cross of Gallantry, a Purple Heart, and the Combat Infantry Badge.

The following is the citation for Richard's Award of the Bronze Medal (Second Oak Leaf Cluster) with "V" Device for the Snake River battle:

For Heroism in connection with military operations against a hostile force: Captain Carlile distinguished himself by heroic action on 6 September 1969 while serving as Assistant District Advisor, Duc Long District, Chuong Thien Province, Republic of Vietnam. On this date Captain Carlile accompanied the 988 Regional Forces Company on a multi-unit search and clear operation. While approaching a woodline, the unit suddenly came under intense fire from a well-entrenched enemy armed with machine guns, automatic weapons, recoilllless rifles, and rockets. During the initial volleys, Captain Carlile was seriously wounded. In spite of his condition, he rapidly assessed the situation and called for air strikes and artillery fire until the radio was destroyed by small arms fire. Under cover of the fires he directed, most of his comrades were able to take shelter in some nearby houses. Realizing the urgent need for communications and despite the severity of his wounds, Captain Carlile further exposed himself to heavy enemy fire while moving to the house in which a Vietnamese radio operator had taken refuge. There he was able to reestablish communications and continued to direct artillery and air strikes until the enemy was forced to withdraw. Captain Carlile's courageous actions averted the almost certain decimation of his unit and turned a possible defeat into victory. Captain Carlile's heroic actions were in keeping with the highest traditions of the United States Army and reflect great credit upon himself and the military service.

Clay Peacock

Clay Peacock was a radio operator during the Vietnam War. His main job was to be the ground contact with aircraft on their bombing and other missions. Radio operators like Clay played an integral role in directing and coordinating these planes as they headed toward and were participating in the missions. He was in contact with several pilots as they were being shot down. Clay was awarded a Bronze Star for heroism during one battle in the war.

My name is Jay Clayton Peacock. I was born November 5, 1947, in Fort Payne, Alabama. My parents moved to Scottsboro after I finished the first grade. I grew up and went to school here. After graduating from high school, I went to Northeast Community College the first quarter it was open. I lost interest after about a year and was about to get drafted, so I joined the Air Force. I was twenty years old.

I did my basic at Lackland Air Force Base in San Antonio, Texas. Basic training in the Air Force is not as intensive or as long as in the Army. I was only there for six weeks, and basically they taught military protocol, how to march, and so forth. After basic, you typically are assigned to a technical school. In my case, I went to Keesler Air Force Base in Biloxi, Mississippi, for radio operator school. I was there around four or five months and received a permanent assignment at Maxwell Air Force Base in Montgomery, Alabama, with the 2047th Communication Squadron. I stayed roughly eighteen months.

I went to Vietnam on September 25, 1969. I flew into Cam Ranh Bay and stayed for three or four days until I was assigned to go to Natrang at the Direct Air Support Center, which provided support for the 1st Field Force, Vietnam. It was called DASE Alpha and was a 24/7 operation. We controlled a lot of the air strikes in the II Corps Area. I was there a couple of months. They broke us in on the radios, learning the lingo and how things actually operated. It was shift work, and since I was one of the new guys, I worked the three-to-eleven shift, which turned out to be one of my favorites. When the planes came down, you did the arrival and logged the hours and maintenance. I also worked with preliminary night defense, spookys, and shadows (AC-119 gunships) which came in handy later on. The spookys were WWII cargo planes converted to gunships early in the Vietnam conflict. Most of them had four mini-guns mounted on one side so the plane had to fly in a bank to shoot because the guns were fixed. They also dropped flares. Some of them only went on flare missions at night to give the guys on the ground some light. I gave these planes a ground contact, coordinates where they were going, and what the situation was where they were going. We were the ground contact. We also took their after-action reports that consisted of time on target, ordinance expended, and results.

After Natrang, I went to a beautiful little place called Gianghia. It was a 23rd ARVN Division outpost in the Ban Me Thout area. I think about 120 Americans were there. We had a couple of artillery batteries and a Forward Air Patroller Team. I was part of TAC, or Tactical Air Command. There were two or three radio operators at different times. Air Force Intelligence was also there with four pilots and two flyable aircraft, along with four Army pilots who had a couple of flyable aircraft. Our pilots flew missions in support of the South Vietnamese division. The Special Forces advised the Mike Force, which we supported. Mike Forces were indigenous forces made up of local tribesmen and led by Green Beret (Special Forces) soldiers. There were usually three or four of them with each unit.

I was running radios on the ground. I had to make contact with the aircraft at least every thirty minutes. When they found something they needed to shoot up, they would call me and say a set of fighters was needed at a certain location, or something like that. I would pass the coordinates on to the Direct Air Support Center and tell them what I needed. They would clear the coordinates (make sure no friendly forces were in the area) and come back to me with information on the number and type of planes they were sending, along with what kind of ordinance would be available. I would also be informed of the contact frequency and estimated arrival time. I would tell them how to contact the forward air controller. There were three radio sets that could be used. We had Fox-Mike or FM, VHF, and UHF. FM was real short range, as was UHF, and they were used between the aircraft. One plane would fly around and mark the target with marking rockets so the fighters could make adjustments like how far to go west or to string from west to east.

The planes we used were O-1s, or Oscar-1s, which were observation aircraft. Our unit also had O-2s, but these were mostly used with paved air strips. They were two-person little prop observation planes that were "tail draggers" and looked like Piper Cubs with four marking rockets on each wing. The marking rockets were white phosphorus rockets. When they hit the ground, a big plume of smoke was visible and acted as a marker. They usually flew at about 1000 feet, but it wasn't unusual to see them at about 600 feet. They were supposed to be over 1500 feet, but couldn't work effectively that high. Once the bombers would see the mark, they would come in and say "I'm hot", drop the bombs, then pull up and roll away. Another bomber would come in, maybe from another direction. They did not come in front-to-back because that would give the bad guys time to line up on them.

The kind of bomb depended on the situation. It could be cluster bomb units, which were several hundred hand grenades. Most of the time, though, they would be 500, 750, or 1000 pound high explosives. The napalm was egg-shaped and rolled and started fires. Only rarely were more than two of these used because TAC was watching and would make corrections, such as "you were 400 meters long on that one and you need to come 400 meters back". Then the second plane would come in and try to adjust for the 400 meters. The fighter planes only had fifteen minutes to get on their way. The target could be anything like enemy troops, trails, bunkers, or buildings in addition to supporting ground troops. The strangest targets I know of were elephants, which were used by the enemy as pack animals. It was similar to how we used to use mules around here when they would drag logs from the top of the mountains. When the log was unhooked at the bottom, the mule knew to go back up to the top. The elephants pulled sleds that might hold mortar rounds or whatever on them. The sleds were covered. That is why the elephants were bombed.

I was at Gianghia for about three months. I did go out some with the planes. Normally the pilots would fly with a Vietnamese interpreter in the back seat or with Special Forces guys or intelligence people. The intel people had cameras and did what was called a visual reconnaissance. They had a set area they worked and went out to look it over. They were very familiar with the area and knew where every hooch and trail was. When in the back seat, you were basically another set of eyes for the pilot. He might be looking on one side and you the other. I didn't fly a whole lot, but I did fly some to see what it was like. When they started getting shot a lot, I didn't manage to go up as much. We didn't lose that many planes, but we had a lot of them shot up, mostly by small arms fire. Since these were almost like Piper Cubs, a 30mm round would do some damage. The worst thing to be hit with was a 23mm radar-guided anti-aircraft shell that the enemy shot at jets. The only thing that saved the pilot and observer was that the small recon planes were so flimsy these 23mm shells could go through the wing root and on up over the plane, so shrapnel from the explosion fell from above the aircraft. With metal wings, the explosion would have happened nearer the occupants and could cause more damage to them. I have a tape recording of that happening to my boss. The guy in the back seat was on his first combat mission. He was a new forward air controller. The plane got shot, but they made it back to the base and landed. The plane couldn't get off the ground to go anywhere, and it was destroyed later.

While I was there, I slept in a hooch with two-man rooms. The bunks were very small. We did have running water, which was nice, so you could take a shower. There was a little Army chow hall, and the cook prepared food for the air crews and Air Force people and the Artillery guys.

After I left Gianghia, I went back to Nha Trang, but our unit was about to move to Pleiku. So two or three of us were sent there to get everything set up. It was called II DAS, or number two Direct Air

Support Center. This was part of the restructuring that was going on. When I was there, it was toward the time in 1970 when Vietnamization was very active. A lot of Americans were not being replaced, and we were supposed to be training Vietnamese to take our place. I did train one guy, Nuyen Van Maanx, who was actually from North Vietnam. His family had escaped to the south when the communists took over the north. He spoke fluent English, French, and Cambodian.

At Pleiku, I was strictly a radio operator, working the second shift because I just liked to. It was basically what I had been doing, but we did do some special operations in support of certain missions that were going on. These were usually Special Forces groups that were out and had high priority for air support should they get into trouble. We kept a pretty close eye on them. Also, there were some outposts up there. One outpost was under siege for three to four weeks, and we lost three air-supply aircraft and the crews.

Yes, the places where I was were under fire at times. I spent three nights at a little place called Bu Prang, and it was under siege for about thirty days. I pulled nights out there, and we had enemy get on the camp with us. Special Forces guys killed five of them one night I was there. That was the only real hard combat I was involved in, those three nights. The camp got hit a lot with indirect fire like mortars and stuff like that. We took 150 rounds of incoming fire in fifteen minutes at one time there.

Occasionally, we would be in a convoy and have a radio. Usually we would be in contact with a pilot who was covering us. We had snipers a few times, and we would empty out our M-16s. If there was an area from where we thought we had been fired on, we'd open up on it.

I was in the Pleiku area until I came home, which was September 31, 1970. I didn't take any R&R, so I was basically seven days a week the whole time. We would have a day off occasionally, but it wasn't very often. When we lived in Natrang, our hooch was in the Grand Hotel compound, which was an old French hotel. The hotel is where the general lived, and our radio room was in the compound, which was right across the highway from the South China Sea. So we could go to the beach and lay out in the sun.

I had some unusual experiences while I was over there. I ran into two guys from here. Walter Hayes was stationed at Cam Ranh Bay and lived across the street from the radio area. Eddie Arnold was a guy I went to high school with, and when his colonel came to Cam Ranh Bay, he would be there for three or four days. He would stay with Walter, and I was able to have a steak with them one night. Eddie was killed here at Revere, where we worked together.

The hardest thing I had to deal with was someone saying over the radio that a plane was in trouble. When the pilot got hit, he would say "I'm taking hits, I'm taking hits", or "My engine is on fire", "My hydraulics are down" or things along that line. Usually they would try to make it to a certain point and give me an approximate location of where they were headed, like to a clearing about 500 meters away, for instance. Of course, you would notify everybody else in the area to watch out because this guy was going down. I have on tape when some of them were shot up. We lost the three air supply transports, we lost a helicopter, and we had one O-1 that disappeared, in addition to the ones that were shot up. I knew the pilots well. We lived with them and ate with them. They had their own hooch, and ours was right next door. I am still close to some of them today and keep in touch, and I have been out to Texas to see my commander that I worked for over there.

He is the reason I have the Bronze Star for Valor at Bu Prang, which I mentioned before. The day before this incident I'm going to tell you about, it was another radio operator's turn to go out. We rotated every three or four days. He told us the night before that he was not coming back because he thought he was going to get hit. He packed his stuff up. One of the hardest things to do was pack up another person's things to send home. The next day he got hit by a 57mm recoilless shot that took his shoulder off. We never saw him again, because he was taken straight out of the country. He did survive. Because of his injury, they needed somebody else for Bu Prang, and I told Major Lattin I would go. I got my 16mm and ten bags of ammo. They said they needed more maps, so I rolled some up and put them in a knapsack-thing and went to the airfield. There was a CH-47 that was going out. The CH-47 is a two-engine transport helicopter that will carry over twenty people. It had a load of Vietnamese rangers on it. I ran up to it and told them where I needed to go. The load master put me in the back.

It wasn't very far to go, maybe twenty minutes. On the way, the load master briefed me. He was the one that took care of the loads and the unloading, staying in the back of the aircraft. He told me they had taken the Vietnamese out there once, but they wouldn't get off, and chances were they wouldn't get off again. I told him I had to get in to Bu Prang, and he told me he would get me there. We started to make our approach to Bu Prang, which was a Special Forces camp like a firebase, and the camp was taking fire from mortars, light artillery, rockets, and stuff.

The pilot told us the enemy was hitting the chopper pad, and he asked me if I really needed to get off, and I told him I did. He said he couldn't land and would just have to hover about three feet and I could get out. I was passed this word from the load master, and he told me you will feel the aircraft settle once, and you have to go the second time it settles. The chopper had a tailgate that dropped down and a ramp that you could drive vehicles up. He dropped the ramp down. I felt it settle the second time, and I got off. I wasn't three feet up, it was more like fifteen feet. I hit the ground and rolled. The chopper had a J-97 Westinghouse on the back of it, and when he swung the back end around, I got caught in jet wash. It blew off my steel pot, which was my helmet, and I had to go run it down. Then I had to make my way back to a bunker of some sort for a place to hide. This gave just enough time for the enemy to move the mortars around, so they zeroed in on where I was. I made it to one bunker and then a second. When I got in that one, a Special Forces guy was there. He asked how I got hit already, and I told him I wasn't hit. He said I was bleeding. I looked down and saw I was wet all the way down the front of my knee. I had shrapnel embedded in my knee, and I don't know what happened. There was so much shrapnel around that I probably fell on some of it.

Other US troops were there but weren't close, out in the perimeter. The Special Forces guy pulled some shrapnel out and put a butterfly on my knee. He told me the lieutenant was down; he had been hit before I got there. The lieutenant had armor on the front and back that laced together on the side, but he got hit under the arm from shrapnel from a 57mm or 75mm recoilless rifle. It collapsed his lung. When I got over to where he was, they had already hit him with some morphine. He wasn't functioning, so I took the radios he had and started working the perimeter to get some air strikes in. Actually, I had initially gone there only to assist him with the radio. I worked the gunships and fighters and forward air controllers until it quieted down a little bit. Then I went to the command post where the main radios were.

This was a Special Forces camp, and they were all built the same. The control room was about fifteen feet underground. The entrance was L-shaped, and the passage-way went down and made a right angle turn to the door. It was made this way so somebody couldn't throw an explosive against the door. I stayed there, working the spookys, which protected us at night. I was there for three solid days. Like I said before, the enemy got on the camp with us one time and killed five in the camp. We lost several Montagnard guys, hill peoples who were mercenaries and worked for the Special Forces. Good guys. After three days, the enemy was pushed back, and about 300 of them were killed.

What I did after I landed in the LZ that one day is what a lot of the guys did almost daily. The chopper pilots might fly two missions a day and get shot at constantly. The Special Forces guys were out there all the time. I was there three days and got to go back and take a hot shower. They had been out there for weeks and hadn't had anything hot to eat. You feel a responsibility or brotherhood with the others, but that was just your duty. At night, when we got a lot of our hits, the only way a spooky could support you was to have visual contact. So the way he would find you was for us to kick out flares. We also had strobes we carried in our vest so in case you got hit you could be located.

At Bu Prang, I had one of the strobes when a spooky came. We were getting hit hard, and Bu Prang was lit up like Christmas trees. Because of fog and smoke from all the rounds, the spooky couldn't get a good location on us. He could see roughly where we were but needed a better pinpoint. So I took my strobe light out and got in a trench about chest high. I ran down it, put the strobe out, turned it on, and ducked. The pilot said he couldn't see it. I knew what had happened then, because when you turn that thing on the enemy zeroes in on it. So I turned it off and moved it a little closer to an overhang. I put the strobe on top of the overhang and turned it on and ducked again. Spooky told me he had a tally on me and could see. Now we didn't want to keep using the strobe or the enemy would start zeroing in again. Since it was high up, I didn't want to reach up and get it. So I found a stick and knocked it off, but it fell in the trench. When it hit, there was fire from everywhere coming in. I made it back to the command post, and the spooky covered us good that night. If it was hot like it was that night, they would bring in another spooky after two or three hours.

Around the Bu Prang Camp, there had originally been three fire bases; Mary Jane, Kate, and Helen, named after the provincial commander's three daughters. They were in the path of the NVA, or North Vietnamese Army, and it was hardcore NVA troop territory. This was the NVA unit that attacked the US troops in the movie "We Were Soldiers". We were fighting the same troops they were fighting. Anyway, these firebases were being overrun, and Kate had to be pulled out and evacuated. They had to escape and evade during the night with bad guys coming over the wire. Their leader was Captain Bill Albright, or "Chicken Hawk", who was in Special Forces. He led the twenty-four or twenty-five people around the jungle to meet with friendly forces, losing only one man, which was amazing. I was at Gianghia then, and we were talking by radio to "Hawk", providing coverage with aircraft and trying to keep from pinpointing his location to the NVA units. He was what I consider a real true American hero. I met some of the other Special Forces guys later, and I was honored to be around men like that.

An interesting aside to this. The plane I was working with so much was a spooky-1 or spooky-2. Years later I was working at Redstone Arsenal. Veterans have a tendency to hang around together. I overheard a conversation where someone was saying about when he was on an AC-47. So my ears perked up, and I asked him who he was with. He had flown a spooky at Bu Prang while I was on the ground there. He turned out to be the crew chief of the spooky I talked to so many times. I bought his lunch in repayment for all he had done for us those nights. It was one of those emotional moments that will stay with me forever.

How I finally got the Bronze Star is a long story. Back in that time, when you got put in for medals, it might not go anywhere. In the early 2000s, when the internet was getting popular, one of the first things I started doing on it was search for people. One of these was Major George Lattin, who was my boss in Vietnam. I found him out in Texas, and we started emailing. I found out he was getting a medal from the Army side for the same operation I was in at Bu Prang. So my youngest son and I drove to Texas to see him get his Silver Star, which was awarded to him by a four-star general, Hal Hornberg, who was a 1st Lieutenant when I knew him. While I was out there, George asked me if I had gotten my award. I knew I had been put in for one but hadn't ever heard anything about it. You didn't pursue things like that. He told me he had put me in for a Silver Star and that he still had the paper work and would run it through. So he started going through his congressman. He also got in touch with one of the pilots who had been a witness to the original paper work. They filed it, and it went through Congress in 2005. It was downgraded to a Bronze Star with "V" for Valor. It is not unusual for these to be downgraded because of the thin line between the requirements for the Silver and Bronze Stars.

When I got the Bronze Star, they asked me where I wanted it presented, and I told them on Veterans Day in Scottsboro so my family and friends could be there. Major Lattin drove up here to see the presentation. He died the next October.

I flew back from Vietnam into Seattle. They had us in a reception area. We were told about all the protests going on and that the protesters wanted to catch one of us doing something to one of them by trying to provoke us, but we should stay away if we could. We had seen some of the news about what was going on, but we had no idea how people really felt. When I flew into Los Angeles, protesters with signs were outside and calling anybody in uniform all these names and all that stuff. I upgraded to first class, and the ticket agent told me I should change to civilian clothes, which I did. I didn't have any problem in Huntsville because they were looking for somebody in a uniform and because I weighed 119 pounds. I had weighed about 150 when I went in. I made up for it. I weigh 190 now.

I was assigned to the personnel office as a runner at Tyndall AFB in Panama City, Florida, working on my early out. I had it made there, and the commander basically told me he didn't want me hanging around the office if I didn't have anything to do, but to make sure he could get in touch with me if he needed me. I did things like go pick up his kids after ball practice as a runner.

I did get my early out to go to school and was released six months and twenty-one days early, in February of 1971. I went back to school at Northeast Community College. I went for a couple of quarters. Revere came to Scottsboro, so I went there and stayed for eleven years in general plant work. I have been at Redstone Arsenal since 1996 as a computer technician in the intel and security division.

My military career meant a lot to me. I met people I never would have met in Scottsboro. I grew up during that time, learning to take responsibility. As far as my feelings about the war are concerned, as it says on the brochure, "Ours is a just cause". We were there to help people. Some of them wanted help, some didn't. I worked with some good Vietnamese and some bad ones. But it was the teamwork that was important. We weren't successful over there because the politicians wouldn't let us win it. We were never defeated in battle, only by running and pulling out. It is hard to say if it was worth the cost. Some of the things we did were, but all those guys died for nothing. It was the wrong place at the wrong time. So I have mixed feelings about it. I know that I will probably some spend time back there each day from now on. I guess that is just part of having been there.

Note: The citation accompanying the award of the Bronze Star (with Valor) to Jay C. Peacock is as follows:

Sergeant Jay C. Peacock distinguished himself by heroism as Ground Radio Operator, 21st Tactical Air support Squadron while engaged in ground combat against an enemy of the United States at Bu Prang, Quang Duc, Vietnam, from 26 October 1969 to 28 October 1969. During this period, the Special Forces Camp at Bu Prang came under siege by the North Vietnamese Army. During the siege, Sergeant Peacock was deployed by helicopter into the camp under heavy mortar and small arms fire. The camp was under constant artillery, mortar, and small arms fire. On the second day of the siege, the Officer In Charge was wounded and could no longer function. Sergeant Peacock had to divide his time between his radio operator duties and taking care of the wounded officer. At dusk on the second night, it became obvious the North Vietnamese were making a full effort to overrun the camp. Their position had to be marked for the supporting aircraft. Completely out of marking flares, Sergeant Peacock, using the strobe light from his survival vest, crawled out of the bunker into the open and line of fire to provide the necessary marking of the friendly position. Because of his aggressiveness, the aircraft were able to repel the attack and the enemy withdrew. By his heroic actions and unselfish dedication to duty, Sergeant Peacock has reflected great credit upon himself and the United States Air Force.

Johnnie Byrd

Johnnie Byrd served two tours in Vietnam. His first tour was in 1965 with the 173rd Airborne, which was the first Army ground combat unit in the war. His second tour was in 1970 as an Army operations officer. Later, he had a variety of assignments until his retirement as a full colonel after almost twenty-five years of service. During his tours in Vietnam, Johnnie received two Bronze Stars, a Joint Services Commendation Medal, an Air Medal, an Army Commendation Medal for Valor, and seven other National Defense and Vietnamese medals.

My name is Johnnie Paul Byrd. I was born on June 8, 1939, in Pineville, near Bay Springs, Mississippi, but was raised and went to school in Laurel, Mississippi. After graduating, I went to Mississippi State College, which is now Mississippi State University. I wanted to go into engineering, but we couldn't afford it. I did get a scholarship from a local lumber company and was able to get a degree in forestry.

At that time, two years of ROTC was required in land grant institutions. I liked it and decided to go into advanced ROTC my last two years. I did well and was offered a regular commission in the Army. So after graduation I was commissioned as a second lieutenant in the Army Artillery. That was on 28 May of 1961.

Afterwards, I had almost three years in the 101st Airborne Division, where I went to parachute school, jump master school, and Air Delivery School, making over thirty jumps. I enjoyed all this because I was a gung ho lieutenant. Being in the 101ˢᵗ Airborne was great. The 101ˢᵗ was a pentomic division that had five maneuver battalions comprising three infantry and two light armor. The division artillery had five batteries, and each battery had five 105mm howitzers. The lieutenant's pay when I went in was $222 a month, then I got an extra $110 a month in jump pay as long as I made the training jumps at least once every three months. It was a really good unit of elite soldiers and officers. While in the 101ˢᵗ, I held positions of forward observer, battery executive officer, and battery commander. During this period at Fort Campbell, Kentucky, I met my wife, Carolyn, who was a Red Cross social worker in the hospital there. We married in the post chapel in October of 1963.

I did have a harrowing experience there on my fifteenth jump, which was a full combat gear night jump. There are several things you check: count, check your canopy by looking up, and make sure nobody is close to you. Well, I jumped but didn't get the parachute shock that you would normally get. When I looked up to check my canopy, I couldn't get my head up because my risers were all twisted right down the back of my neck. I was straining pretty hard to get them separated so I could check the canopy. I had what is called a cigarette roll. So I had about two-thirds of a full canopy with air rushing out of the side that was rolled up. I was descending really fast. Other aspects of training are to learn to relax, keep your knees and feet together, and so forth. All this training paid off. There was a little wind, and the air coming out of one side of the canopy was pushing me in one direction. When you have a partial malfunction, you can't just pop the reserve chute. If you are falling slowly, it will fall down between your legs and get tangled all around you. They teach you to take your left hand and hold the reserve chute, then with your right hand pull the rip cord and throw it away; feel which way the wind is blowing on your cheeks; and pitch your canopy out with the wind. So I popped the reserve, and about that time I hit the ground. But I had remembered to keep my feet and legs together and relax the harness. I made a left rear landing. I was bruised up, black and blue from my ankles to my shoulders, and could barely walk. I was on quarters for about a week, but nothing was broken.

A career military officer is trained to go to war. I was lucky, or unlucky depending on how you looked at it, that we had a war while I was in the military. It wasn't fun, of course, because I was away from my family during my two tours in Vietnam. This is the way it happened in my case. I went from the 101st Airborne Division at Fort Campbell to the 173rd Airborne Brigade on Okinawa. The 173rd, the US Army Pacific Reserve, was a very elite unit. A brigade is smaller than a division, and in the 173rd there were three infantry battalions, a cavalry troop which was light armor with self-propelled antitank weapons, and a field artillery battalion with three 105mm batteries. That was supposed to be a three-year accompanied tour, so Carolyn went with me, and we shipped all of out household goods there. I went in January of 1964 and she followed soon after. In May of 1965, the decision was made to send the brigade to Vietnam. General Westmoreland was the Military Assistance Command Vietnam (MACV) Commander. He said something like if they gave him the brigade, he would end the war in six weeks. So we went over there on a temporary change of station, supposedly for about this six-week period. While we were on temporary change of station, we had to make training jumps, so I made my 41st and 42nd jumps in Vietnam from a Huey helicopter.

Some of the brigade left Okinawa on the first of May. Most of the troops flew over, and the artillery, which I was in, went by ship on one of those flat-bottomed Navy boats. I left on 7 May, and my first son was born on the 28th of May back in Okinawa. So I had gone to a good unit in the Pacific, and it turned out they were wanted in Vietnam. The 173rd was the first Army ground combat unit to go into Vietnam. The Marines had some units there, and Army advisors were already in the country.

When we went over, I was the fire direction officer for the artillery battalion. We had Australian and New Zealand artillery units attached to us who would fire coordinated missions with us. The fire direction officer runs the fire direction center, which is where the calculations are made to direct the fire of the artillery in support of the ground forces. I was in charge of that. Our base camp was in Bien Hoa, but we were usually out in the jungle, not there. A lot of the operations we had were in what was called War Zone D north of Bien Hoa. Zone D was just a large area of land basically controlled by the Viet Cong in which we ran "search and destroy" operations, and it was part of the Iron Triangle. In some cases, we did not even have to leave our base camp to fire support. In the next couple of months or so, we were mostly in the Bien Hoa area. Later, we bounced all over the place, even going as far north as Pleiku several times. But I never went to the Delta.

On many of the operations, we had to convoy out into the jungles in order to set up a fire base to support the maneuver units. I was not a "ground pounder" out beating the bushes all the time. We were usually behind them. In Vietnam, of course, there were no front lines, so regardless of where you were, you had to establish a perimeter to afford protection from attacks.

Most of the time when we had an operation like that, the ground forces would go into a landing zone. The infantry troops would be taken in by helicopter, and a lot of the landing zones were hot because the enemy was shooting at them. Sometimes trees had to be cut down to clear the landing zone so the helicopters could land. Our cavalry troop had self-propelled antitank vehicles, or SPATS. They had to go by road since they couldn't be lifted in. The artillery would either convoy up close enough for support or do it from the base camp if we could. There was a wide variety of ways it could happen. After the troops were put in, the mission might be to "search and destroy", secure certain terrain, or whatever the operation was. The artillery was put in a position close enough to offer supporting fire. With 105mm howitzers, we had to be within fifteen miles, but we were usually a lot closer than that. The 105 was called that because of the diameter of the projectile in millimeters. The infantry had their own mortars (81mm and 44.2 inch) they carried with them.

There was no guesswork when we fired the howitzers. Calculations for artillery fire support are intricate. Back then we had a big chart gridded the same as the map we and the soldiers were using. You know the coordinates where you are and your troops are. The forward observers with the maneuver units keep updating this information. So you know where the frontlines are. When they call for fire, they call it in for a specific coordinate, out in front or left or right or whatever. So in the fire direction center you know where you are and where they are, and you have a definite procedure to measure the azimuth and the distance or range. You have to consider the atmospheric conditions with meteorological data you enter into the equation, such as rain, air density, and wind speed and direction. Using all this information, you calculate the range from you to the target, the direction from you to the target, and the atmospheric conditions you have to go through to get to the target. There are different powder charges, maybe up to seven, to choose from. Each of the guns has a sight on it, and the chief of firing battery gets all of them synchronized to make sure they are pointing in the right direction. So from the fire direction center, you give the gunners the azimuth to set the guns on, charge to use, the elevation to achieve the range, and so forth. On larger artillery weapons, a specific powder charge must also be determined.

In our artillery battalion, we had three firing batteries of six 105mm howitzers each. Depending on the operation/mission, one or all three batteries might be deployed. Howitzers within a battery were usually spaced 30 to 50 yards apart, and batteries could be close together or miles apart, depending on the mission and the deployment of the units being supported. You always want to hit what you are shooting at, but artillery weapons are generally used to saturate an area with explosions and shrapnel to neutralize the enemy forces. The killing range of the explosions and shrapnel depends on the type of shell and fuse; the type of soil and how soft it is; how thick the jungle is; how protected the enemy forces are; etc. Usually the forward observer will adjust the fire of one or two howitzers as close to the enemy as possible before calling for "fire for effect". At that time, the entire battery or the entire battalion will fire multiple volleys at the target. The number of batteries and the number of volleys fired depends on the size, strength, defenses, and tactical importance of the enemy target.

The projectiles look like a great big bullet. They can have timed fuses, which are not the most accurate. There are proximity fuses which go off in the air just above the ground, which means the shrapnel is coming at the enemy from above. Impact fuses explode when they hit the ground. There are various kinds of ammunition, such as high explosive ammunition, white phosphorus ammunition, anti-tank, and smoke. The white phosphorus makes a really white billowing smoke cloud and causes fires. A lot of times, especially in jungle terrain where it is hard to determine exactly where you are, there is a procedure where the forward observer just says to fire center of sector. You would then shoot white phosphorus well in front of the observer, and he can make adjustments from where it landed.

Forward observers (FO) were usually artillery lieutenants and stayed with the company commanders. Fire support officers (FSO) were usually artillery captains and stayed with the maneuver battalion commanders. The FSO assisted in planning supporting fires for ground operations, and could call in artillery fire and even air strikes during an operation. Many times there were Air Force forward air controllers (FAC) with the higher level commander, or in the air over the operation area, to direct air support missions in support of the operation. Sometimes we would even provide an air observer for an operation. I flew in a little Piper Cub as an air observer in several operations. That was kind of scary because you would be flying along and see muzzle flashes in the jungle below, and you knew that someone was shooting at you.

When we first went to Vietnam, we were fighting the Viet Cong (VC). However, on one of the early operations, we realized we really were in a war. We lost thirty or forty troops in the upper part of War Zone D, and the enemy troops were North Vietnamese. So the North Vietnamese Army (NVA) units were in Vietnam in 1965.

As the fire direction officer, I was in charge of the group of people who were making all these firing calculations. I had several non-commissioned officers, and about fifteen artillery men in all in the fire direction center because of twenty-four hour shifts and so forth. It was my responsibility to make sure that we were calculating correctly so we could provide accurate fire support to the troops. I had been trained in how to do all of these calculations. The first school I went to in the Army was the artillery basic course, as it was called at that time. That is where we learned all the survey and fire direction techniques, how to be a forward observer, how to adjust fire, and all those things associated with being an artillery officer. When I went in, air defense artillery and field artillery were both logged under artillery. For this basic course, I went to Fort Sill, Oklahoma, where the field artillery was located. Then I went to Fort Bliss, Texas, which is where the air defense artillery was located. After completing that phase, I had to make a decision whether I wanted my career to be an air defense officer or a field artillery officer. I selected the field artillery.

In Vietnam, I was under fire several times, but only once was I in a situation where I was in severe peril. The first six months of my first tour, I was the fire direction officer for the artillery battalion. Then I was moved up to brigade headquarters as an operations officer, working in the brigade's tactical operations center (TOC). We were the folks that ran the operations center that controlled all the operations in the field. I was a captain at the time and was the junior officer on the operations staff. So lots of times when they would send out a small contingent of ground forces, they would want to send out a small contingent from the brigade operations center. That would be me, since I was the junior officer, and two or three non-commissioned officers. On one of these operations, in January of 1966, we went up into War Zone D on a typical "search and destroy" mission. The troops were lifted in, and we convoyed in and set up a brigade headquarters area. The first night we went into a perimeter around the headquarters. The cavalry troop was there along with one company of infantry troops and some Australian units. During the night we were attacked. The enemy was firing in mortar rounds and probing the perimeter. The VC were between us and the infantry troops, who were further out. There was no front line. I didn't go outside much, but you could see tracers flying all around, and the self-propelled anti-tank weapons were shooting, and mortar rounds were coming in. You know, it was pretty hairy. But that is what you are trained for. I just stayed at my post in the headquarters area and coordinated all the stuff that was going on. In fact, I got the Army Commendation Medal for valor during that operation. But I do need to say that this was nothing like being out on the front lines where there were hundreds of VC or NVA shooting at you, but it was still hairy.

I also had the responsibility of writing the after-action reports after each operation. Basically, it was a summary of the operation. I'd have as appendices to this report a copy of the operations order directing what we were going to do and any supporting documentation. It was just a kind of summary of how the operation went. I was able to do that because I had access to the logs at the operation center where we were keeping track of the operation. This was the last six months of the first tour.

The living facilities depended on where you were and how much you wanted to dig yourself in. When I was in the artillery battalion area, I slept on a cot in a small tent with three or four others. We had a bunker where the fire direction center was located at the base camp. We dug down and used sand bags to make an elaborate bunker. At the brigade headquarters, we had a larger tent and bunkers. We might use wood pallets to get us off the ground. I was there all four seasons, but I don't remember the weather or bugs being really bad. It rained hard sometimes but I don't remember that being a real problem, and we had bug repellent for the bugs. But again, I was not out in the jungle all the time like the infantry Of course, we had field latrines, and we rigged five-gallon water cans for showers. In the hot sun, the water got pretty hot and made for a good shower.

The VC had mortars, but the NVA did have artillery support, and they certainly fired at us. In fact, at Bien Hoa, they blew up an ammo dump. It was a big loud explosion with a big fire and lots of smoke.

After my first Vietnam tour, I went to the field artillery advanced course at Fort Sill. That was just additional artillery training at a higher level and lasted about a year. Then I went to McNeese State College in Lake Charles, Louisiana, as assistant professor of military science in ROTC. That was about a two-and-a-half-year tour. It was very enjoyable. The worst part of that tour was that I had to serve as a survival assistant officer, which meant I was one of the people who had to go out and notify folks that their loved ones had either been killed or captured or were missing in action. That was tough, really hard, but is something that has to be done. We tried to make sure it was done in a dignified, professional way, with as much consideration for the families as you can. As I said, it was tough, but other than that, the tour was fun. I was teaching young ROTC students and served as officer-in-charge of the rifle team.

I was promoted to major while at McNeese State, and then I went to Command and General Staff College at Fort Leavenworth, Kansas. Again, that is more senior schooling than I had in the advanced course. Here you were trained to be a commander or staff officer at higher levels. From there, I thought I might be assigned to the Washington, DC, area, but to my surprise, I was selected to go back to Vietnam again.

This time I was assigned to the 7th Air Force Headquarters at Ton

Son Nhut Air Base in Saigon in Army operations working with the Air Force. I went to work about six o'clock at night and spent most of the night writing the orders (called frag orders) for all the close air support sorties provided in Vietnam by the 7th Air Force the next day. I would also review all the operations for the day just past and prepare a briefing which I gave to the MACV J-3 about five o'clock the next morning. The information for the following day's activities included preparatory strikes, interdiction strikes, air caps (planes that were on station in the air support ground operations), and other special missions. I was there to make sure that the ground forces perspective was included in the decision-making process to determine how best to support the mission. I did not do orders for the B-52 strikes; these were done at a higher level. I did have to track the B-52 strikes and include them in the morning briefings I gave to the MACV J-3 (a Marine Brigadier General at the time), and sometimes the Deputy MACV Commander. My shift ended at six o'clock the next morning. I got my second Bronze Star during this tour. During this tour, I conducted a number of studies providing information used in making decisions affecting air support provided in Laos, Cambodia, and Vietnam.

After Vietnam, I went to the University of Georgia for advanced civil schooling. I had requested to get a meteorology degree because we were always having trouble getting good met data to use in our fire direction. So I requested to go to civil schooling for that, but they came back and said with my forestry degree, it would take too long to get the math and science needed to finish meteorology school. So they said they were willing to send me to Georgia for a masters in business administration (MBA) if I would specialize in automatic data processing. I thought that sounded pretty good, so I went for two years, beginning in 1970.

The Army's plan at that time was to have what was called dual specialties. My primary was field artillery and my secondary was to be data processing. The objective was to let you go to your primary for three years and the secondary for three years. However, they quickly learned that if you were in data processing and stayed out of it for three years, you had to start all over. After Georgia, I went to Fort Belvoir, Virginia, to the Army Computer Systems Command and was involved in developing the Army's Tactical Fire Support System (TACFIRE), which was an electronic automatic data processing fire direction system. I was there about three years, then I went over to NATO headquarters in Brussels, Belgium, where I was the chief of the management branch of what was called the Situation Center. The chief was an automatic data processing position responsible for developing the automatic data processing system in NATO headquarters in support of all their operations. The chief was the personal advisor to the System Manager of the NATO internal command and control system. He was also technical advisor and provided administration support for the NATO Headquarters Information Systems Management Board, composed of representatives from twelve countries. While there, I developed the first automation security program for NATO's worldwide computer network.

That was supposed to be a three-year assignment, and it would have taken me that long to finish all the work that was needed there. But I was selected for battalion command, so we were only in Brussels for one year. I went from there to Wiesbaden, Germany, to take command of the 2nd Battalion, 20th Field Artillery. This was a 155mm Mechanized Artillery Battalion. The howitzers were bigger than the 105s I had been used to, and they were mounted on tracked vehicles, similar to a tank. We had three firing batteries of six guns each, a Headquarters Battery, and a Service Battery, for a total of about 750 officers, non-commissioned officers, and artillerymen, along with hundreds of vehicles. This was the culmination of my artillery career. It was what I had been trained to do for the first sixteen years of my career. We were the direct support artillery for the Corps Covering Force with general defense positions in the Fulda Gap on the East German border, which was the location most strategists thought the attack would come if the Soviet Union ever attacked. We had nuclear rounds for our howitzers, and we had our full basic load of ammunition, which we had to guard at all times. If there had been a confrontation with the Soviet Union, we would have been right in the middle of it.

When I came back from Germany, I went to the National War College ,which was for senior level schooling. This college is a unique military school. The Army, Navy, and Air Force all have war colleges, but the National War College is a combination. We had classes smaller than the others, but mixed. We had forty Army, forty Air Force, and forty sea services, which included the Coast Guard, Navy and Marines. There were also forty civilians from governmental departments. A large percentage of people who go to the National War College wind up making general officer. That was one of those decision points in my career. Carolyn and I had to decide what we wanted to do the rest of our lives. In order to go on and do what you need to do to become a general, I had to go to the Pentagon. That is absolutely the worst working environment that there is. I knew I was going to make full colonel since I wouldn't have been sent to Senior Service School if they hadn't been planning to promote me. Carolyn and I made a conscious decision that we were not going on that route. I went over to the Computer Systems and told the Commanding General I would like to come back over there, knowing full well I was probably taking myself out of competition for general.

So I went back to the Army Computer Systems Command (CSC) and had a number of positions, including Chief, Data Services Division; Director, Operations, Security and Plans; and Command Inspector General. That was an interesting position. There is an old saying in the Army that the inspector general comes around and always says he is there to help you, but it doesn't normally turn out that way. I thought this was really a great opportunity to help people, because if there were some regulation you were supposed to follow that didn't make sense, I was in a position to change it. I had that position for over a year, and was promoted to full colonel during that time.

From CSC, I went to be Director of Computer Operations at the Army Military Personnel Center (MILPERSIN) in Alexandria, Virginia. We had a very large computer center and a network connecting all the Army posts, camps, and stations around the world. From there, we controlled all the movements and assignments of Army personnel around the world. While there, I supervised the wiring of the entire command to connect every desktop to mainframe computers. Today, most of that would be done wireless, but then we had massive cables made up of thousands of small copper wires.

It was there that we decided to leave the military after almost twenty-five years. I was looking at Computer World magazine and saw a position in Morgantown, West Virginia, as Director of West Virginia Network for Educational Telecommuting (WVNET). They had a computer center in Morgantown with connections to sixteen public colleges and universities around the state. I applied for the job. The interview process was grueling since they had many questions and concerns about a military guy and because I only had a masters degree, not a PhD. I got the job and was there three-and-a-half years.

West Virginia University was also in Morgantown and was WVNET's biggest customer, and I had gotten to know the people there. The position of Vice President for Computing and Information Resources WVU came vacant. I applied and went through another grueling interview process. Afterwards I was told there had been 158 applicants. Dr. Franz, the Provost who later became President of the University of Alabama in Huntsville, called and asked me to come over. He said he made the final decision and wanted me to tell him why he should hire me. Having worked across the street and being familiar with the WVU department, I told him what I thought should be done. He did hire me, even though he knew he would get a lot of flack because I had no PhD. I took the job in September and got a Christmas card from him that December thanking me for proving he had been right in hiring me. We stayed in WVU until 1996, when we came to Sand Mountain.

My feelings about the Vietnam War are that I was trained to go to war and to carry out orders of the Commander-in-Chief and lower commanders. At the time, I thought we were doing the right thing. After many years of reflection, I do not think it was worth it. Also, we did not seem to learn a lesson from Vietnam when we went into Iraq.

Note: Johnnie Byrd received two Bronze Star Medals for his service during the Vietnam War. The Bronze Star Medal citations are as follows:

By direction of the President the Bronze Star Medal is presented to Captain Johnnie P. Byrd, 094171, Artillery, USA, for distinguishing himself by outstanding meritorious service in connection with ground operations against a hostile force in the Republic of Vietnam during the period May 1965 to April 1966. Through his untiring efforts and professional ability, he consistently obtained outstanding results. He was quick to grasp the implications of new problems with which he was faced as a result of the ever changing situations inherent in a counterinsurgency operation and to find ways and means to solve those problems. The energetic application of his extensive knowledge has materially contributed to the efforts of the United States Mission to the Republic of Vietnam to assist that country in ridding itself of the communist threat to its freedom. His initiative, zeal, sound judgment and devotion to duty have been in the highest tradition of the United States Army and reflect great credit on him and the military service.

By direction of the President the Bronze Star Medal (First Oak Leaf Cluster) is presented to Major Johnnie P. Byrd, United States Army, for distinguishing himself for meritorious service in connection with military operations against a hostile force during the period July 1970 to June 1971 while serving as Operations Officer, Tactical Air Support Element, Air Operations Division, Office of the Assistant Chief of Staff for Operations, Headquarters, United States Military Assistance Command, Vietnam. During his tenure Major Byrd demonstrated truly outstanding initiative and professional competence in the coordination of all matters concerning close air support in the Republic of Vietnam with the major ground units and the Director of Operations and staff, Seventh Air Force. He displayed exceptional competence, logic, and intelligence in the performance of these extensive and demanding duties. His period of service occurred during a time when the Joint Air Ground Operations System in Vietnam was especially complex and challenging. He met this challenge in a responsive, dynamic, and imaginative manner. By virtue of his keen insight and exceptional understanding of the proper application of close air support, he was able to make timely recommendations and accurate forecasts of impending operations to his superiors. Major Byrd's performance of duty was in keeping with the highest traditions of the United States Army and reflects great credit upon himself and the military service.

For his Vietnam service, he also received a Joint Services Commendation Medal, an Air Medal, an Army Commendation Medal for Valor, and seven other National Defense and Vietnamese Medals.

Isaac Ashmore ────────────────────────

Isaac Ashmore was a crew chief in an assault helicopter unit in Vietnam, going on hundreds of missions depositing and picking up troops in hot landing zones. He was shot down seven times on these missions. His unit had the highest kill number but also the highest number killed during that time. He received the Distinguished Flying Cross and multiple Air Medals for his service.

My name is Isaac Newton Ashmore. I was born in Scottsboro on June 29, 1948, and went to school here, graduating in 1967. This was the last class to graduate from the old high school. Afterwards, I went to work at Campbell Oil Company for a short time before I was drafted into the Army in July. I went to Fort Jackson, South Carolina, for basic training, and then to Fort Rucker in Ozark, Alabama, for aviation training on helicopters like the Huey. I was there for a few months.

From Fort Rucker I went back to Fort Jackson for in-country training before I went to Vietnam. That was to give us some idea about what it was like there before we went. I knew nothing about the country of Vietnam before then and had no idea about what I was going into. I had heard about the war and about the protesters. I also knew that a lot of people about to be drafted were going to Canada, but that was not my way of thinking. My feeling was that if I got drafted to help my country, that was what I was going to do. I wasn't really much worried about being sent to Vietnam.

I went to Bien Hoa, but didn't have any orders after I got there. I stayed about four or five days at Bien Hoa before I got them. I asked them to send me back home, but that didn't work, so they sent me to Vung Tau, which was the in-country training center, instead of back home. My job was to do head counts at night of those in for R&R at the base. I had to keep up with their names to make sure they got back. If they didn't, I sent the military police to find them. So that is what I did the first six weeks.

Then I got orders to go to Bear Cat, a fire support base between Vung Tau and Saigon off Highway 1. I can remember getting on my first helicopter after I got to Vietnam. We went at a low level, just above the trees, and some guy said he hoped we didn't get any fire. I asked myself if I was going to get shot right off the bat, but we made it to the base. It was not hot when we landed, but about every two or three nights we would get in-coming rounds. It was a well-fortified fire support base. I was stationed at Bear Cat as my base camp for the rest of my term in Vietnam. The 80th Australian unit was at the base. A bunch of Korean work teams were also there, and they were mean head-hunters.

Bear Cat was in the southern part of the delta between Vung Tao and Saigon in the middle of a rubber tree plantation with a lot of trees. The base probably covered about twenty acres. A small transportation unit was also there that would fly to Saigon or Vung Tao to pick up supplies for us that helped run the fire support base. A big berm was around the base. Also, there was wire all around it that would cut you up if you tried to go through it. In each corner was a big tower with machine guns and full-time guards for security. Since we were in a rubber plantation, it was more open and like a farming area. At least the jungle didn't come up right to it. One time during the Tet Offensive, the enemy tried to overrun the base but they never did. I was not there at that particular time. Pretty often, though, we would get mortar fire or rockets at night. Sometimes people would get hurt, particularly if the rounds hit in the barracks area. I think one time a couple of guys got killed while I was there.

When we were at Bear Cat, there was a mess hall where we ate. Our barracks were like two-story chicken houses. We lived off 3.2 beer and water, which we didn't have much of, when we were out on missions. We took two or three cases of beer with us every day, along with C-rations, on these missions. We ate in the field or while flying or whatever. Oh yeah, we made sure we had the beer with us.

I was in the 240th Assault Helicopter Company, 1st Aviation Division. They attached us to different units to provide support. At first, I was with the 9th Infantry Division. We worked all around, like in the Delta, Saigon, south of Saigon, and east of Saigon. We even went into Cambodia. I can't remember when that was; I just know it was before the Tet Offensive. During this time, we were going into Cambodia every day from Bear Cat. We would leave out early in the morning before daylight. We didn't wear any nametags because we weren't supposed to be there, but we were.

Our mission was to go to other fire support bases in our area and pick up troops and put them out in landing zones. We had enemy contact about every day. We would put troops into areas where they were needed, then move out of that area and put troops somewhere else. We might pick them up two or three hours later and again move them. It seemed like we were just moving them around all day long. Sometimes we must have gone on ten operations a day, and I probably went on at least four hundred or more during my year over there. We even provided support for the gunboats that ran the Mekong Delta. Those gunboats patrolled the river and tried to cut off any guns or anything coming in through the delta. The guys on these boats were sitting ducks. Anybody on the bank could pick them off as they were going by. If they had made contact with the enemy or had boats that had run into the bank and they had to jump out and run, we would bring in troops and put them out. These troops' job was to run down the enemy. We might even pick up troops from tank units, and sometimes the tanks would be in a circle like in wagon trains. I think I only went on three or four missions at night.

I was crew chief of the helicopter. My job was to take care of the copters and maintain them. I made sure they were ready to go every day. In our company, we had a maintenance team that would fix the helicopter overnight if it had anything wrong with it. I made the decision the next day on whether it was ready to go. On the helicopter, we had a pilot, co-pilot, gunner, and myself as crew chief. But the guys rotated out and in all the time. I fired weapons, too. We had 60mm machine guns. I was a gunner when I first got there, teamed with a crew chief to learn what was going on. Then I took my position as crew chief.

The pilot I was with had been in Vietnam a long time. I think it was his third tour. We flew lead helicopter, the first to go in; then we would go back up and circle around and come back to pick up anybody that might have gotten hurt when they got off. The pilot would call in fire support if it was needed, like Phantoms or gunships or mortar or whatever. One pilot was Richard Street, but we called him One Way Street. He was about twenty-two years old and he was crazy. He smoked more pot than they had in Vietnam. We had radio stations we could pick up in our helicopter, and there was a great big speaker on the front of our helicopter. When we started into a landing zone, he would turn on that music wide open, and it sounded like it was coming from everywhere. It was unbelievable. I saw something like this on some of the movies out later. People would say they couldn't believe they really did that, and I would say that we did. With those 60s firing and that radio wide open, we would scare the VC half to death.

Landings in the hot zones were touch-and-go. Sometimes the troops would have to jump out maybe ten feet off the ground. As a matter of fact, we went back to pick up people up who broke legs this way, especially if it was a hot zone. We took a lot of fire. I remember that once we set down in a landing zone over close to Cambodia where I think there must been a whole brigade of enemy soldiers in the tree line. At least it seemed like hundreds. That is one of the times I got shot down, out of seven total. In other words, the particular helicopter I was on was shot down seven different times in the landing zones.

When we got to a landing zone, we would either get a command to fire off the left side or the right side or both sides. Sometimes when we were coming in, we would have Cobras or other aircraft on each side of us as we were going in. They would be laying down fire as we landed. The first helicopter in always dropped smoke, too, by throwing out canisters. That would give the guys cover as they got off the copter. It would also give us cover in the helicopter because the swirling of the blades made it so the enemy couldn't see to shoot us inside. They might be shooting some heavy automatic gunfire at us. We had our chicken plates, which was a big thick armor that slid over and covered the front and back. When you sat down, it would sit on your legs. But most of the time we took the back shield out and sat on it to keep bullets from hitting when shot from below us. Sometimes we wore headgear. I figured out right quick after seeing some of the guys that got hit that a good .22 rifle would shoot through them. Actually they were only good for impact if you had a crash to keep you from busting your head. Lots of the time we just wore a cap or nothing.

In the movies, it shows the gunners standing on the outside of the helicopter, and that is the way it really was. We would ride out on the skids, even at 2000 or 2500 feet, without anything holding us. If you slipped, you would fall, so it was a stupid thing to do. We had lanyards to hook for safety, but we didn't always use them because it was too much trouble to try to move around. Your ammunition was behind the pilot but the grunts, or infantry guys, were sitting around all over the floor. When you tried to move over or around them and try to get ammunition or whatever, untying that thing just didn't work well. Yes, we did receive fire when we were out like that, but I never got hit.

We would carry eight infantry guys. When we picked them up, it would be four on each side. When we were in a hot zone, we would load as many of them as we could get in and get out quick. But eight was the normal number. That is a good load when you count the four of us, too. Eight troops being discharged doesn't seem like it would do much good, but when you have six helicopters, they add up.

We would be shot down because they might shoot the main rotor blade or into the fuel system, and one time the pilot got shot and crashed us. It didn't kill him. Two other times something happened to the pilot or co-pilot that made us go down. Once we were down for just a short period of time after the co-pilot got shot. We pulled him out of the seat into the back so the pilot was able to get to the stick so he could handle the helicopter. If we got shot down in a hot area, we would have another helicopter come in and pick us up. Two times we actually had to get out on the ground and stay for a while. The infantry guys we had already put out covered for us. We had Cobras and Phantom jets come in, as a matter of fact too close one time. It was close enough so that when the bombs exploded, it almost took your clothes off. If it was close enough you could see the pilot and look him in the eye, you knew he was close. You hoped that pilot was dead-on. Absolutely, you could feel the concussion. You could stick your fingers in your ears and it still was loud. I was lucky because I never was injured when we went down.

The Cobras were strictly gunships with mini-guns underneath that would rotate. I think they had 22mm guns and had rocket pods that held about twelve on each side. The Hueys were only used to haul troops, and that was what I was on. Most of them had a 60mm caliber machine gun hung by a bungee cord on each side or on a tripod on each side. On the lead helicopter, we would have twin guns stacked on each other, so you could have two guns shooting at the same time. We knew to fire in the tree line or in the base of the tree line. Sometimes if a group of helicopters had already flown into the landing zone and put in troops, those copters would drop smoke into the area where they had received fire so we would know where to fire.

Some of the landing zones might be dry rice paddies or even wet rice paddies. There might be cleared-out areas where B-52s had dropped bombs, or wooded areas might be cleared to make room for the landing copters. We would drop out the guys whose job was to clear the area. There was no set size for the landing zones, but I have been in them when the blades would hit the trees, and I've seen them clipping limbs off trees many times as they were getting out of the zone. I guess that normally, though, the zones might be a hundred to a hundred and twenty-five feet wide. You didn't want to go into a place where you would tear your rotor blades off. You also wanted to be able get away quickly because the enemy was usually lurking in that area. I would say that at least eighty-five percent of the time we received fire in the landing zones.

Once while I was with the 9th Division, we went into what is called the Plain of Reeds, which is over by Cambodia close to the delta, where the enemy was infiltrating out of Cambodia. It was an area that had grown up in elephant grass and tall reeds, which were almost like fishing cane. The area had been sprayed with Agent Orange, and everything had died and burned off. It was just a black soot burned-off place. You could see in the daytime the trail over which they moved at night. We would carry troops to the wood line in places like this and usually pick up enemy fire.

I was in Vietnam during the Tet Offensive. During that time, we mostly flew around Saigon, usually giving support to the troops on the ground. We did what is called paper-cup bombing. We took the little paper cups you drink out of and put a phosphorus grenade in them, pulled the pin out, and dropped them out of the helicopter. When they hit the ground, the cup would bust and the grenade would go off. If you had thrown it out from 2500 feet, it would go off way before it hit the ground. We were burning some of those villages down where the NVA was in the outer skirts of Saigon. During the Tet Offensive, we did have orders at times not to fire unless we received fire, because we were in downtown Saigon or around more civilized areas. But the rest of the time, this was not the case, in part because we were fired on so often in the landing zones.

In the latter part of my stay in Vietnam, we were working with the 1st Cavalry, which moved from up north near to the DMZ, and we went up to help them move down close to Saigon. This was in the latter part or after Tet. We went into a landing zone and the pilot, co-pilot, and gunner got shot. The gunner almost fell out of the helicopter. We were in a Huey. We were in a real hot zone and had other helicopters come in. We got these guys who had been shot out of the seats. I had flown a helicopter quite a bit, getting on the stick and flying with the pilot or co-pilot, like at the end of the day. We were not supposed to do that, but you know how it goes. Anyway, I had done this enough that I could take off and land pretty decent.

When they got shot, we were actually on the ground. We had come into the landing zone and touched, taking all that fire. Two or three of the infantry soldiers inside had also been shot, but not real bad. Anyway, I was able to fly that helicopter out and landed in another landing zone. We were able to get them to a hospital.

From August of 1968 to 1969, my helicopter unit had more kills than any other aviation unit in Vietnam. They called us the "Greyhounds". We also had the most guys in our unit killed than any other aviation unit in Vietnam. This is according to some of the statistics they gave us. I attribute my not getting shot to good luck and the good Lord being with me. I lost two good friends that got killed.

On another mission, we flew the Beach Boys on an in-country trip in the southern part of Vietnam. They went to several areas. As a matter of fact, I went with them to an R&R center in Vung Tau from

Saigon for them to put on a concert on the beach. We also flew the Safaris, which was a big group back in the sixties. These flights were real memorable. I had a hat that I got signed, but I think it got lost before I even came home. But flying those groups was a real big deal. I got to see Bob Hope one Christmas over there. We weren't supposed to go, and we weren't supposed to have a helicopter. But we went to the flight line, and the crazy lieutenant and some others of us flew from Bear Cat to Saigon to Bob Hope's Christmas Special. We got into trouble over it, but not bad.

I saved my R&R and went to Hawaii for a week to meet my mother and dad. This was in the latter part of my tour. Other than that time, I was doing missions mostly out of Bear Cat. Also, during my time with the 1st Cavalry, we sometimes stayed at their fire support base and did some missions from there. They had bunkers where we could put our helicopters in. They had old metal stuff we could land on. There were big berms around them for protection from fire. We might stay overnight after flying all day. They had barracks to catch a nap. If we needed maintenance on the copters, we would have to go back to Bear Cat.

I was exposed to Agent Orange. We had some Hueys that were rigged with the big tanks that sprayed Agent Orange. I have ridden as crew chief on one of the helicopters spraying Agent Orange around the Plain of Reeds and over in that area. What we would do on what we called our days off was if somebody needed something, we'd help or swap out with another copter, and that is how I happened to be on the ones that were spraying. We flew as low as we could when we were spraying. I have been where we'd make turns and come back over where we sprayed, and the stuff would be swirling around the blades. I never was sprayed directly, but with the fumes and being around it, I'm sure I was exposed. We were spraying the foliage and not aware of the harmful effects of it. I was diagnosed two years ago with prostate cancer, and prior to that I had breast cancer. Before then, I had never signed up for benefits or anything. When I was diagnosed with the prostate cancer, my doctor suggested I be tested and checked, since Agent Orange lingers in your system. They even say it can be carried on to your kids. I'm receiving benefits now for the prostate cancer.

I got back from Vietnam in 1969, then went to Hunter Air Field in Savannah, Georgia, spending the rest of my time in the helicopter division, training troops going to Vietnam. Then I came back home and went back to work at Campbell Oil Company for a short time before going to work at Gibson's Department Store. In February of 1971, while at the department store, I got a letter saying that I had been awarded some medals from Vietnam that I didn't even know I had been put in for, and that a military guy was coming over from Redstone Arsenal to award me these medals. I got the Distinguished Flying Cross based on my saving those lives during the mission when I flew the copter out and for saving the life of the gunner when he almost fell out of the copter. I don't know how many Air Medals I received. We got one of these for ever so many hours we flew on combat missions. They would have an awards day in Vietnam, and they would hand them out and you would just put them in a bag. I also got some after I had been out of Vietnam.

I stayed with Gibson's for two years, then went to work with the Scottsboro Electric Power Board. I retired from there after twenty-five years as a lineman. I served on the Scottsboro city council from 1996 to 2004.

To be honest with you, I enjoyed my experience in Vietnam but wouldn't want to do it again. I want to go back one day and see what the area looks like now. I lost some good friends there. I thought the South Vietnamese people were caring, and they liked us. They didn't enjoy what was going on because they had been fighting for years. I don't have bitter feelings about them at all. We didn't have much contact with the South Vietnamese soldiers. They seemed almost like us in that they didn't want to be doing that either.

My thought about the war itself is that it was a political war. We didn't really need to be over there. I think the Vietnamese could have handled their own problems like they had been doing for many, many years. They called it a conflict, but it was more a police action forced on us young guys for no reason at all. No, I absolutely don't think it was worth it. We could have had a different aspect about the whole thing, and it would have come out a lot better. If we had gone over there to take care of the thing and get it over with, we could have cleaned the place up and come back home and not lost as many of our men as we did. It was just a drug-out action. We would go into one area and take it and then give it up and have to go back in and take it again. We were just getting our guys killed and killing other people.

Bernie Arnold

Bernie Arnold joined the Air Force when seventeen years old and trained as a jet engine mechanic. He spent over five years in Washington maintaining and repairing the Air Force One presidential plane, advancing to a supervisory position later in that tour. He then spent five months in Danang at the end of the Vietnam War as a supervisor in the jet engine branch. Bernie retired from the military after twenty years of service. During this career, he graduated from high school and earned a college degree.

My name is Melton Bernard Arnold. I am called Bernard or Bernie. I was born in Chester, Georgia, which is in Dodge County, on April 30, 1936. My daddy was a farmer and a mechanic, and in 1942 he went to work with Warner Robins as an aircraft mechanic. My grandfather had worked there during WWII. We moved to Macon, and I was actually raised there from about six years old. I went to school in Macon, but I dropped out at the age of sixteen.

After that, I worked in construction for about a year, then decided there was a better way in life than handling a shovel. I had an uncle who was a career military sergeant, and he kind of enticed me to join the service. He had a pretty good life in the Army. So I started thinking about the Air Force and thought I might be a jet engine mechanic, since I had always worked on my cars. Besides, I had worked in a garage when I was sixteen years old. When I went in, I asked to be a jet engine mechanic, and sure enough I qualified and wound up a jet engine superintendent before I retired after twenty years. I had gone in when I was seventeen and stayed until I was thirty-seven years old.

At first I went to Lackland Air Force Base for basic training, then to Chanute Field in Illinois for jet specialist training. After that, I went to Pine Castle Air Force Base, which is an international airport now, just outside Orlando. From there, I went to Barksdale Air Force Base in Louisiana and stayed about a year. At this time, they were making up some new wings for the Strategic Air Command, so I asked to go with a cadre instructed to set up the wing at Homestead Air Force Base in Florida. In 1956 we went down there, and in 1957 we helped form the 379th Bomb Wing of the Air Force.

There were no medical facilities set up at the base at first, so all wives were asked to work at the city hospital, James Archer Smith Hospital, to take care of our medical needs. My wife worked there as a nurse and medical technologist. We only had one car, and my wife had it. I had a Vespa motor scooter to take me to the base and back home.

During my tour of duty at Homestead, we were deployed on temporary duty to Sidi-Slimane Air Force Base in French Morocco, North Africa, for training in desert conditions with our B-47 bombers. We were there over two months. The weather was hot in the day and cold at night. I celebrated my twenty-first birthday in Morocco, but it was just another workday. Over two months in the desert was enough for me.

I was stationed at Homestead a couple of years and re-enlisted. In 1958 we went to Lockbourne Air Force Base in Columbus, Ohio, which is now Rickenbacker Air Force Base. From there, I went to Brize Norton base in England. We were tenants on a royal air base. We took care of B-47s that were ready to go to Russia or wherever. These were loaded with atomic bombs or hydrogen bombs. The crew was on a moment's notice to take off. We did have one RB-47 that was shot down over Russia. My wife was with me in England, and we adopted a daughter, Angie, over there.

In 1963, we were sent to Pease Air Force Base in Portsmouth, New Hampshire. While I was at Pease, I started going to college at the University of New Hampshire and later to the New Hampshire College of Accounting and Commerce. It is now called New Hampshire

Southern. I graduated from there with a BBS in 1967. BBS means a bachelor of business science. We adopted a son, Randy, while at Pease.

When I was first in the military, I was a mechanic at a 1 level. I rose up through the 3, 5, and 7 levels and on through the 9 level and retired as an E-8 Senior Master Sergeant with a propulsion superintendent designation. On a day-to-day basis early on, I was a "wrench bender", out there every day fixing engines and changing engines and doing whatever needed to be done. I worked for eleven years on the B-47. After that, I worked on B-52s, 707s, DC-140s, DC-131s, and many others. I was repairing the planes until I got up to the supervisor level, where I supervised mechanics and was responsible for them. I had to sign off their work, which signified the plane was ready to fly.

In 1967, I was chosen to go to Andrews Air Force Base in Washington to work on Air Force One. I was selected because I was a quality-minded person and because I would do the job right. Also, I had just gotten my college degree, which probably had a lot to do with it. Not only did I work on the Air Force One, I worked on all of the presidential fleet, which was about forty planes at that time. Air Force One had the number 26000 and was only called Air Force One when the president was on board. The tail numbers of the others were different. There were different types of planes, such as little Jet Stars, 140s, and so forth that took the vice-president and others around. President Johnson's and Nixon's families got to fly on these quite a bit. Their daughters were in college at the time, and they would take them there and bring them back home on the planes.

President Johnson kept a King Air plane there, and we maintained it for him. I never saw him fly on it during the five years I was there. All the two people who were assigned to it did was shine that plane and keep it ready to go.

I flew on one of these planes only once. It was a backup which looked like Air Force One with the same 26000 number. This one was used for various purposes, such as to carry reporters and security people. The reason I flew on it was because they wanted us to check out some engines.

The inside of Air Force One was very nice. It had good

accommodations very fitting for the president. It had a living room, separate bedrooms, and eating facilities, just like a nice hotel room.

When I first went to Washington, I filled in as a mechanic even though I was an E-6 on orders for E-7, and I put on my Master Sergeant stripes soon after. But I went there as a "toolbox" mechanic to work on Air Force One and the others. For a while I worked different shifts, then the occasion came up for me to be a shop chief. I took that position, and later I was the branch chief of the reciprocating engines, propellers, and jet engines areas. I was propulsion superintendent for all of it for a while. About the last year I was there, I was asked to take care of the department called deficiency analysis, which was an investigative-type situation. Any time a part failed on the planes the president or vice-president would fly on, I would have to go out, secure the part, talk to the mechanic, write a report, send the part to a facility, get a report about what the problem was, and then write another report or get a verbal report or both as to what happened and what could be done to prevent it from ever happening again. I gave the report to the chief of maintenance. We hoped it would never happen again. They didn't want anything to fail on Air Force One.

My five-plus years in Washington was a control tour. That means that when they select you for a job like that, you get to stay for at least five years unless you mess up. If you do your job well, you get to stay for the full five years. I knew that when my time was up, I was open to go to Vietnam since I had served all those years without going. I left Washington in September of 1972 and went to Danang Air Base in Vietnam, and I was there about five-and-a-half months before the treaty was signed.

I didn't do any physical maintenance on anything while I was at Danang. I was responsible for the whole branch, which consisted of the jet engine shop, the reciprocating engine shop, and the propulsion shop. We had some little forward air patrol planes, but a special group of people worked on those. Even though I didn't do any maintenance, I was responsible for those that did do it.

It was fairly calm around Danang as far as the war was concerned. Danang was known as "Rocket City", and we would receive rocket fire whenever the Vietnamese chose to do so. Usually around midnight they would send in about ten of them. So many rockets had hit that place over the years that many things had been blown up.

One of the fellows took me around the base, and he showed me the barracks down near the flight line. We went upstairs into a room and there were holes all around. He told me rockets hit outside. I told him I didn't really think I wanted to live in that room. Anyway, he said he had other places, so I became a resident of the main compound in a little safer area. It was nice, close to the mess hall and the NCO club. It wasn't that I didn't want to stay with those troops, but it was safer away from the planes.

I was never real close to where the rockets landed, maybe a hundred or so yards away. If you are that close, it could still kill you from the splash. It makes a big hole where it hits, but it depends on the trajectory of the thing. If it comes in at an angle, most of the junk will fly out in one direction but not so much the opposite direction. The explosive on the rockets was about fifteen pounds of TNT, and it would blow a big hole. If it hit a barracks, it would do severe damage because of the concussion, and if it hit a plane, it would set it on fire. We had some planes that did catch fire this way.

I went there in September of 1972 and left in March of 1973, about the time it was over. When they signed the ceasefire, there was supposed to be a forty-five day period in which neither side would fire, but the enemy was free to set up rockets if they wanted to. Our security people would fly up and see what was going on. The day before the peace treaty was signed, one of these security men who lived in my barracks came to me with tears in his eyes. He said if they didn't sign the peace treaty the next day, the Vietnamese would shoot those rockets at us. It was estimated that 8000 rockets were all around the Danang facility. He told me that they could blow us away. He was afraid for his life, and I was afraid since he was. Really, that was the only day I was scared. The next day the peace treaty was signed. Twelve hours after it was signed, they shot those rockets over Danang, five minutes of it. We took cover, and I got a recording of it but can't find it. I had timed and dated the recording, so that if they killed me somebody would know what happened. I don't think it was ever reported over here that it occurred.

I took cover that day in bunkers behind our shop that we could jump in. We also had revetments around the buildings. These are actually little walls. Around our shop we built them out of ammo cans filled with sand and stacked into little walls. I hired the Vietnamese on the base to fill them with the sand and stack them up. A rocket could hit from twenty to thirty feet away and that wall would help protect us from the splash. We had a little coffee shop that made money, so I could pay the Vietnamese. Actually, I had two of them that worked for me all the time. The revetment around the barracks I lived in was a long wooden box about four feet tall that was filled with sand. Some of us even went further than that. We filled sand bags and put them under our bunks. Any time we heard the sound of the rockets on the PA system, we were to take cover under anything we could.

While I was at Danang during the cease fire, there was little for us to do, just taking care of the things we were supposed to, like getting ready to leave. We had money available, so we had some parties. Our coffee shop made the money. I had inherited it since it was in my branch, and we sold coffee and donuts. It was open to everybody. We hired a Vietnamese lady to be the server. It would make so much money we didn't know what to do with it, so we would have those parties with it. Since you couldn't pocket the money, you had to spend it. The guy I inherited it from told me you could have a party about every month, cooking steaks out and all. I asked where he got the steaks, and he said from the Vietnamese. Then I asked where they got them. It turns out they were stealing them from the chow hall and then selling them to us. I said I wasn't going to be a part of that, but we still had parties. I knew a master sergeant who knew how to cook pinto beans, so everybody who wanted to eat pinto beans and cornbread could come and eat with us at the barracks on Friday nights, even the base commander. One time they forgot to invite him, and he told us about it. We didn't forget again. Little things like that make the world go a little easier. To me, it was not all war. Some of it was fun. The clubs had some of the best entertainment you've ever seen.

I had a little interaction with the Vietnamese. I think there were four of them that worked with me, training to be engine mechanics and propeller mechanics. In addition, I knew some of them around the base that spoke a little English. One or two of them could speak very good English. The man who worked for me didn't speak much, but the lady that worked in the coffee shop did. She was married to a Vietnamese lieutenant. You could talk to these people and find out what was going on instead of our government's version. We could get their side. I remember a young lady who worked in the typewriter shop, which was near mine, who knew what was going on in the outside area. They lived outside but worked on the base. There were some ladies of the night called cyclo-girls because they would come onto the base at night on their bikes. I didn't mess with any of them, and I even told my wife that.

In early 1973, our own forces bombed us at Danang. It was a huge mistake. I was on the MARS station talking to my wife when the bombing occurred. MARS was a radio station that would transmit like a telephone. You would talk, then say "over", then the other person could speak. If you got your name on the list you could go early in the morning or late at night when the airways would permit communications to cross. This MARS station was hooked in with Barry Goldwater's residence in Arizona and was manned in the basement of his home for the duration of the war, at least in Danang. It might have gone somewhere else in other parts of Vietnam. That was how Goldwater did his part in the war, and we are thankful to him for that. The only thing it cost us was the phone call from Arizona to home.

Anyway, when we were bombed, some of our aircraft were to rendezvous at a certain point and then go and bomb the targets. Well, the word got mixed up and the rendezvous point became the target, and this target happened to be Danang Airbase. I don't know how many bombs were dropped, but they destroyed three of our fuel dumps that the Vietnamese had been trying for years to destroy. They burned for three days. The fuel tanks were like those big vats you see along the highway in several places. I think one Vietnamese was killed, too. But I know what 500 pounders sound like now. It shakes the earth.

One of the housing lieutenants asked me if I would take charge of the senior NCO barracks that I lived in. It was just an extra duty, and it did kill time, so I accepted. There were five or six Vietnamese ladies that took care of cleaning the barracks. I would collect the money from the residents and divvy it up between the workers. I would go to American Express and get Vietnamese money in exchange for our scripts and distribute it. Well, one day a year they have what is known as "boss day", and they want you to sit in the floor and eat with them. I came into the barracks that day and there was the worst smell I have ever been around. I found the ladies sitting down waiting for me. The ladies said the smell was from a fish sauce, a fermented fish sauce. I couldn't bear to taste it. I did ask then not to ever bring that into the barracks again.

When the treaty was signed, we were given forty-five days to vacate the country. If you had been in-country for less than six months, you were reassigned to another place in Southeast Asia. If you had been there over six months, you got to come home. People were going every which way, and I was responsible for 120 people at that time. I had to help get those situated going to the other places, so I was kind of busy for a while.

I have to admit that I never touched an American weapon while I was in Vietnam, but I was given a captured AK-47. I had to turn it in because it was forbidden to take them home.

They asked me to go to a little place called NKP, which stands for Nha Kon Phanon, in Thailand. They told us we would finish the war from there. It was a nice little duty station. I was responsible for all the helicopters and various other aircraft. I spent about six months there. I was very proud that I was asked to come back to Washington to do the job I had been doing before, because it meant they respected me enough to ask me to come back. But I did turn the assignment down and asked to be assigned to Warner Robins for retirement. I was there about six months before I did retire. Then I went to work at Coca Cola in Macon, Georgia, as the production manager. In 1977, we moved to Albany, Georgia, where I was the production engineer for ten Coca Cola plants. We moved to Scottsboro in 1990, and I started a new career in real estate.

I am a very proud veteran of Vietnam. I did my job the best I knew how. I would do it over again without question. I just appreciate the Air Force letting me be part of it. I did not encounter any problems when I came back, but I heard that others did. I'm glad I didn't because I would have taken it personally. I appreciate the military and my career in it. They made a life for me. I probably wouldn't have gotten a high school education and certainly not a college degree if it hadn't been for the Air Force, which has been my life.

Ernie England

Ernie England had a remarkable military career. He fought in WW II and in the Korean conflict. Later, he was one of the early American advisors in Vietnam before combat troops ever arrived. Nor were the years between Korea and Vietnam particularly quiet. He spent time at Fort Benning as a member of a small, special operations team involved in clandestine missions that essentially no one knew about. Ernie also spent several years in Germany operating a truck loaded with antennas and other specialized equipment, listening in on various communications. Because of the nature of a significant portion of his military career, the story he was able to relate is somewhat limited.

My name is Ernest Arlee England. I was born in Gadsden, Alabama, on June 26, 1926. The day I turned seventeen I went into the Navy. I was eager to go, and my dad signed for me.

My main job in WW II was piloting landing craft in the Pacific. The landing craft would be loaded with troops, and I would take them close to the beach, unload them, and then go back and get another load. These were the troops that were doing the fighting. If the enemy was not expecting us, there might not be any firing. Sometimes, though, they might already be on the beach, and then it could get rough. And sometimes the first load would be okay, but the enemy would be on the beach by the time I took the second load.

We took about thirty troops and their equipment on each load. The craft had an end that opened outward, and that is where they got off. When it was down, I could see the beach. If I got that far, and if the beach was empty, I felt I would be able to get back. Some of the craft pilots didn't get back, but I did. The ones that were lost usually had something happen when it was least expected.

I was aboard ship near Iwa Jima when the war ended. We got the news on the radio from Tokyo Rose. We often listened to her. She usually told things to dishearten us, but all it did was fire us up.

You see, after the war was over a lot of the soldiers got to go home. It depended on things like how long you had been over, your family, and your age. I was low on that list, so instead of going home, I was assigned to an underwater demolitions unit. I got sent to disarm floating demolitions just off the beaches in Japan. If a ship hit one of them, it was a goner. It was a dangerous job, and some didn't make it. If you did make it, you would get flown home. I got pneumonia when I was doing this job, and I got one of the first pure penicillin shots.

I got out after the war ended. I stayed with my dad a few weeks, but there weren't any jobs to be had. I couldn't stand it, so I went into the Army. I wanted the money, so I joined the Airborne because they paid fifty-five dollars a month more. I took all their training for jumps and all.

I wound up in Korea because they sent me there. My job was doing almost everything. I was a courier for a while. Radios were not used for anything really important. So they had some guys who were messengers, and I was one of them. Sometimes they would send me by plane or helicopter.

I was in some battles in Korea. I also made two jumps. The stars on my Airborne cap are for the two combat jumps. Once we jumped and took over Seoul under fire. The other time was to head off a prisoner train heading through a mountain. The train had a bunch of captured South Korean soldiers and was taking them out of the country. The train passed through a tunnel, and we waited on the other side. There was not any fire this time., but we got the prisoners freed. One of my friends got hung up in a tree on a jump. When they got him down, he had been shot all to pieces. Korea was pretty bad.

After Korea, I was at Fort Benning for quite a while. I was on a special team that did jobs they were ordered to do. All the orders came from some other place. They would tell us when to leave, but we did not know where we were going until we got on the plane. How long we were gone depended on how long it took to do the job. You don't just grab a guy and send him on a mission like this. You have to have the mindset for what you do, ever what it takes to do the job. You need to be a sharpshooter in case of an emergency, but hopefully you don't have to do that. I didn't enjoy what I was doing, but whenever I had one of those jobs, I felt like I was helping somebody. No one knew about our unit on the base except for the company commander. I've never read anything about these operations or heard anything about them. I can't talk about them for different reasons.

I was at Fort Benning for quite a while, then I went to Germany. There I had a big enclosed army truck that had all kinds of electronic equipment. They would tell me where to go in Germany, so I would go there and set up the antennas. They would go up about 200 feet, and I would tape everything they picked up. We were trying to pick up communications. I might be gone maybe a month or six weeks. When I was off, I would go all over. I spent two weeks in France one time. While I was in Germany, I bought one of the first Volkswagons and even brought it back when I returned to the states. My five years in Germany were the best time I had in my military career.

I went to Vietnam before our troops got sent there. I was a Master Sergeant. I was one of just a few advisors in South Vietnam. We flew in. I went around to different South Vietnamese military outfits, teaching them how to do things, such as setting up ambushes and everything to do with the infantry. They would show me how they did something, and then I would show them how it should be done. They learned pretty well and did good. I did not have an interpreter with me, but the Vietnamese had one. Any mistake the troops made, I would write it down. Then we would sit down, and I would draw out for him the way it should be done.

I might be at any one place anywhere from a few days to a week. I was in the jungle. I didn't have a tent; I just slept out in the open. I would dig up a little dirt and that was my pillow. I didn't take much food but would get a food drop periodically. I would tell them where and when. Then when I got the food, I would have to move on because somebody might have seen it dropping. The Viet Cong was pretty active, and I encountered them sometimes and there would be firing. This usually happened on the way to where I was going.

I moved around a lot over there. There were two American officers. No information was given over the air, so they would call me and I would meet them somewhere to get my orders. I wouldn't even tell them where I was right then. There was always the possibility someone was listening in.

One of the worst things that happened in Vietnam involved a Vietnamese guide they gave me. I had a big roll of hand grenades hanging off my belt. These grenades are real fast to use, and you can get to them before someone gets you. Well, every once in a while I would miss one. I just assumed they were knocked off the roll by a bush or something. One night I caught the guide over there where the grenades were hanging, and that was how they were disappearing. I took care of that problem. The Vietnamese officer in charge apologized and apologized about it. That officer is the one who gave me a picture of a Vietnamese scene when I left. (*Note: The scene is that of the Vietnamese countryside. On it is the following inscription: Best wishes to Ernest England, 1*st *Battalion Advisor, and is signed by Captain Do-Gang-Loc of 1*st *Battalion, 49*th *Regiment, 25*th *Infantry Division.*)

After Vietnam, I was sent to Fort Benning and never went overseas again. They gave me a house, and I had it pretty easy there.

I had two injuries while in the military. My ears are bad, and that happened in Vietnam when I got blown out of a jeep that hit a landmine. My vertebrae got injured in WWII. I don't really know exactly what happened. All I know is that I woke up and they sent me to the hospital, and I stayed there a short time. I do know I was walking along the beach in front of my landing craft, waiting for the troops, when I must have stepped on some kind of explosive.

After the military, I worked for the sheriff's office and for the paper mill in Stevenson.

I don't regret my military service. If I needed to, I'd go back tomorrow, doing the same thing, even at eighty-five years old. I just believe if we had a problem, I would go. I just think that a man who lives in the best country in the world should serve if the government needs you and never regret it. If you don't do your part, it is a sad day.

About the Author

Ronald H. Dykes lives in an outer, outer suburb of Scottsboro, Alabama, just inside the fringe of the metropolitan area. This is his fifth book and the fourth in a series on Jackson County history sponsored by the Jackson County Historical Association.